THE RUSSIAN PLAY

AND OTHER SHORT WORKS

THE RUSSIAN PLAY
AND OTHER SHORT WORKS

HANNAH MOSCOVITCH

THE RUSSIAN PLAY

ESSAY

USSR

MEXICO CITY

PLAYWRIGHTS CANADA PRESS
TORONTO CANADA

Playwrights Canada Press
The Canadian Drama Publisher
215 Spadina Avenue, Suite 230, Toronto, Ontario, CANADA, M5T 2C7
416-703-0013   fax 416-408-3402
orders@playwrightscanada.com • www.playwrightscanada.com

This book would be twice its cover price were it not for the support of Canadian taxpayers through the Government of Canada Book Publishing Industry Development Program, the Canada Council for the Arts, the Ontario Arts Council and the Ontario Media Development Corporation.

Production Editor: Michael Petrasek
Cover design: Leah Renihan

Library and Archives Canada Cataloguing in Publication

Moscovitch, Hannah
        The Russian play and other short works / Hannah Moscovitch.

Plays.
Contents: The Russian Play -- Essay -- USSR -- Mexico City.
ISBN 978-0-88754-809-3

        I. Title.

PS8626.O837R88 2008   C812'.6
C2008-903217-9

First edition: July 2008.
Printed and bound by Canadian Printco Ltd. at Scarborough, Canada.

Dedicated to Julie White.

TABLE OF CONTENTS

ACKNOWLEDGEMENTS

For the development of *The Russian Play* I am indebted to Natasha Mytnowych, Djanet Sears and Joanna Falck. I would also like to acknowledge the contribution of workshop performers Holly Lewis, Andrew Bunker, Kara Diamond and Blain Watters. The cast of *The Russian Play* helped me to sculpt the script over the course of our many workshop productions: Michelle Monteith, Aaron Willis, Shawn Campbell and Tom Howell. Claire Jenkins's music, Camellia Koo's various sets, Kimberly Purtell's lighting and Monica Dottor's choreography became part of the storytelling and should therefore be acknowledged here. My special thanks to Natasha Mytnowych for her vision and fearless determination.

Essay was developed with the help and encouragement of Michael Rubenfeld and Maureen Labonté. Kelly Thornton, Ruth Madoc-Jones, Lydia Wilkinson, Vicki Stroich, Natasha Mytnowych, Jonathan Ullyot, David Dean and Caleb Yong also offered me their dramaturgical input. Thank you to William Webster for participating in the Rhubarb! Festival workshop of *Essay*. Many thanks are due to actors Richard Greenblatt, Claire Jenkins and Jordan Pettle for their insights into the script over the years. My special thanks to Michael Rubenfeld for his ambition, faith and love.

Natasha Mytnowych encouraged me to write and facilitated the development of *USSR*. Maev Beaty helped me to craft the production draft of the play and Dina Polyak provided me with a firsthand account of life in Soviet Russia. Alan Dilworth very generously offered me his dramaturgical input during the development of *Mexico City*, as did actors Molly Atkinson, Maev Beaty and Brendan Gall.

I would like to extend my thanks to all the directors, performers, designers and technicians who worked on these plays for years without earning much more than the occasional bottle of alcohol. Organizations and theatres that funded and/or participated in the development of *The Russian Play*, *Essay*, *USSR* and *Mexico City* include: Absit Omen Theatre, Banff playRites Colony, Belltower Theatre, Buddies in Bad Times Theatre (Rhubarb! Festival),

Company Theatre Crisis, Harbourfront Centre (HATCH: emerging performance projects), Nightwood Theatre, Ontario Arts Council, SummerWorks Theatre Festival, and Toronto Arts Council. Finally, I am grateful to Mary Vingoe and the Magnetic North Theatre Festival for presenting *The Russian Play*, and I am deeply indebted to Ken Gass, Colleen Smith and Factory Theatre for producing the double bill of *Essay* and *The Russian Play*.

—Hannah Moscovitch
June 2008, Toronto

PLAYWRIGHT'S NOTES

Sonya's first speech to the audience in *The Russian Play* references the KGB. The KGB served as the Soviet Union's intelligence agency from 1954 to 1991. The play takes place in the 1920s, during the first years of Stalin's dictatorship. I have chosen to use an anachronistic term because it is a popular reference; audiences are generally more familiar with the KGB than they are with earlier Soviet secret police organizations. I take a similar dramatic liberty in *Mexico City*. The play is set in 1960 but the Templo Mayor, the Aztec Temple that is referred to in the text, was not excavated until 1978.

For the premiere productions of *The Russian Play* and *Mexico City*, set elements were minimal. Space was created using lights and sound.

THE RUSSIAN PLAY

The Russian Play premiered at the SummerWorks Theatre Festival (a co-production between Company Theatre Crisis and Absit Omen Theatre) in Toronto on August 3rd, 2006, with the following company:

SONYA   Michelle Monteith
PIOTR   Aaron Willis
KOSTYA   Shawn Campbell
VIOLINIST   Tom Howell

Director: Natasha Mytnowych
Set & Costume Design: Camellia Koo and Natasha Mytnowych
Original Music: Claire Jenkins with Tom Howell
Stage Manager: Julia Lederer

> *The Russian Play* won the 2006 SummerWorks Jury Prize for Outstanding New Production.

The Russian Play was later produced at Factory Theatre in Toronto as part of a double bill with *Essay* in January of 2008, with the following company:

SONYA   Michelle Monteith
PIOTR   Aaron Willis
KOSTYA   Shawn Campbell
VIOLINIST   Tom Howell

Director: Natasha Mytnowych
Musical Director: Claire Jenkins
Assistant Director: Julia Lederer
Choreographer: Monica Dottor
Set & Costume Design: Camellia Koo
Lighting Design: Kimberly Purtell
Original Music: Claire Jenkins with Tom Howell
Assistant Set & Costume Design: Anna Treusch
Stage Manager: Joanna Barrotta
Assistant Stage Manager: Alexandra Stephanoff

CHARACTERS

SONYA: the flower-shop girl, various ages starting at sixteen
PIOTR: the gravedigger, twenties
KOSTYA: the Kulak's son, thirties
VIOLINIST

The characters speak with Russian accents.

THE RUSSIAN PLAY

The VIOLINIST plays The Russian Play *refrain in the darkness. Lights come up on SONYA. She is dressed in a ragged skirt and a shawl. She holds a piece of bread. She picks a hair off of it.*

SONYA   Is a little wet. But is okay. I wish for some vodka to offer to you, but only this bread.

SONYA contemplates the audience.

Ahn! I see what you are thinking. You are thinking this is Russian play, you are thinking Chekhov, Tolstoy, so boring. And Russia. Shitty country. Stalin, Kremlin, KGB. And as you are thinking this, you are looking in program to see if there is intermission when you can leave.

Beat.

No intermission.[1] But, please, let me reassure to you that I am wanting for your amusement, and also your illumination on many subjects. But mostly on subject of love.

Beat.

Ahn! Now I have got for myself your attention. Okay, so, I am wanting to answer for all of you important question. Very important question is… where do you hide piece of bread? Ahn? Where do you hide? In the shoe? Yes? In the shoe?

Beat.

First place they look.

SONYA holds out the bread.

Where do you hide piece of bread? I ask myself this, I am looking for answer, and as I am looking for answer, I am

---

[1] If *The Russian Play* is billed second in a double-bill, and it plays after an intermission, the line can be changed to:

SONYA   Intermission complete….

thinking of girl. She is mistress of gravedigger in small Russian town, Vladekstov.

> *The lights flicker. When the lights come up, the bread is gone out of her hands.*

Ahn yes, the shit lights. I am sorry to apologize.

> *Beat.*

Okay, so, I am thinking of mistress of gravedigger. She is working in flower shop. Beautiful flower shop very close to graveyard. On way to graveyard, many people are thinking, "I would like some flowers," and there is shop, very good for business. Also good for business, girl in shop with nice figure, saying always, "What can I get for you, mister?"

> *Beat.*

Her name is Sonya. And the gravedigger, Piotr. Always the shop owner is saying, "Go Sonya, take these flowers to the church for funeral." And Sonya, she is walking by graveyard, and there is Piotr.

> *Lights come up on PIOTR in a graveyard, digging a grave. SONYA curtseys to him and he nods at her.*

(to audience) And Piotr is saying to her.

PIOTR Hello, Sonya.

SONYA *(to audience)* And Sonya is saying. *(to PIOTR)* Hello Piotr.

> *SONYA watches PIOTR dig the grave.*

Has someone died?

PIOTR Yes. Dasha, the baker's second daughter.

SONYA Oh no, but she was so young and so beautiful!

PIOTR Yes, but not so beautiful as you, Sonya.

> *Lights out on PIOTR.*

SONYA *(to the audience)* So you see how it was between them.

> *Beat.*

Sometime, the shop owner say to Sonya, "Look at these flowers for wedding of Kulak's son. He is marrying that no-good girl, Anya. Always wearing fur, how can she afford? But is his funeral, if he want to marry flashy girl who will spend all his money, then he can have pricy flowers for cheap wife." And Sonya would say, "Don't trouble yourself for taking the flowers. I will take them over to the Kulak's house if you don't like." And Sonya would take the flowers on a long walk all the way to the churchyard where Piotr is digging.

Lights up on PIOTR in a graveyard. She curtseys and he nods.

PIOTR   Hello Sonya.

SONYA   Hello Piotr.

SONYA watches him dig the grave.

Has someone died?

PIOTR   Yes. And if you come a little closer, I will show to you.

PIOTR beckons to her. She looks in both directions and hesitates. He holds out his hand.

Come!

SONYA approaches. He shows her the grave. She hesitates.

Look.

SONYA peers over the edge. She can't see very well, so she leans in.

Don't fall in, Sonya!

He grabs and holds her. She laughs and disentangles herself.

SONYA   Piotr! There's no one down here!

PIOTR   Not yet, no, but soon. Winter is coming. So cold in Vladekstov. So cold, and what to do to warm up?

PIOTR leans in to kiss SONYA. As their lips touch, the lights go out on PIOTR.

SONYA   *(to audience)* So you see how it was between them.

    Beat.

There is song Piotr is always singing, in Russian, but I translate for you. Okay, ahn, song goes….

    SONYA speaks the song, translating.

Laughing, laughing, over the fields
Over the fields, ha ha ha, we go laughing
Until the snow comes
Freezing the river and the sky and the birds
And my love for you.

    SONYA contemplates the audience.

Is better in Russian.

    SONYA sings a little of the song in Russian.

Smee-yom-sya, smee-yom-sya, cheerez pol-ya
Cheerez pol-ya, ha ha ha, mi smee-yom-sya.

    SONYA cuts herself off.

Okay, but think of Piotr singing.

    SONYA sings a few more words of the song. PIOTR enters and sings with her.

SONYA/PIOTR   A kakda Prid-yot sneg
Zam yorz-nit ree-ka, eh nebo, eh pzee-zi
Eh mo-you lyou-bov teeb-yeh.

SONYA   Where did you learn this song, Piotr?

PIOTR   In Moscow.

SONYA   Moscow! When were you in Moscow?

PIOTR   Right after I was in Leningrad.

SONYA   Leningrad!

PIOTR   And now I am in Vladekstov, making new life for myself in new Russia.

    PIOTR smiles at SONYA, holds her.

There is 'nother part of the song, Sonya, and is best part, but you don't sing.

SONYA   What other part, Piotr?

PIOTR   Ahn! Let me sing to you!

> *PIOTR sings to her.*

You are just a little piece of Russia
Sonya, just one little piece
But you are the most beautiful piece of Russia
Sonya, the most beautiful piece.

> *PIOTR sings the song and they dance. Lights out on PIOTR.*

SONYA   *(to audience)* You see? You fall in love with him too!

> *Beat.*

One day, Sonya is singing in flower shop this song of Piotr's. The shop owner, she laugh when she hear and she say, "That is gravedigger's song! Is good song for him." Sonya say, "Yes, because he digs graves is right he sing sad song of love." But the shop owner, she look around kind of sneaky and then she whisper to Sonya, "Or maybe his wife taught it to him. She gives him so much troubles, he'd rather dig graves in Vladekstov than live with her in Moscow." And she laugh at this very funny joke.

> *Beat.*

Ha ha ha.

> *Beat.*

Okay, so, heart of Sonya is broken. But heart is very strong organ. You can rip it out and put it back in again and it still work okay. So what is big problem? Why is Sonya waiting for Piotr to come by with his shovel? Why go and wait in the cold? Why not forget about him?

> *Beat.*

Because… in less than nine months she will have something to remember him by.

Lights up on PIOTR in the graveyard.

PIOTR   Sonya? Why are you standing here? You look so cold!

SONYA   Yes, I am cold, Piotr. I am cold, but your wife in Moscow is colder!

As PIOTR is about to justify himself, the lights go out on him.

(*To audience.*) This is shit part of love.

Beat.

Sonya is stupid girl, yes? She like his stupid song, and she get into bed with him, and now she's this problem. Very stupid. But, when woman is sixteen, she is like…. No, I forget it. Ahn! When she is forty, she is like Europe, because she is in ruins, like America when she is twenty-five, at height of powers, when she is sixteen like Africa, undiscovered country.

Beat.

Undiscovered and stupid Sonya.

Beat.

Ahn yes, and Russia! When woman is sixty, she is like Russia. Everyone knows where it is, but no one wants to go there.

Beat.

Ladies, you can't see, but all the men are nodding.

Beat.

Now Sonya is walking back to flower shop in the cold, she is lying in the cold bed, listening to the cold outside, thinking about Piotr's words. He is saying to her, "Don't worry, Sonya. I won't leave you like this, I will help with problem. Come back tomorrow at the end of the day when Vladekstov is sleeping."

Beat.

All day Sonya is wrapping flowers and wrapping flowers. The shop owner say to her, "What Sonya, you are not
singing? Don't like that song so much anymore?" And
she laugh to herself.

>*Beat.*

Ha ha ha.

>*Beat.*

When the flower shop is quiet, and the shop owner is
sleeping, Sonya put back on her clothes, put back on her
shoes, wrap her shawl around her, and walk to graveyard
where Piotr is waiting.

>*Lights up on PIOTR in the graveyard. He holds his
>shovel and a small sack of tools. He beckons to her.*

PIOTR   Come, Sonya. Lie down.

>*SONYA doesn't move.*

(*gently*) Come.

>*SONYA doesn't move. PIOTR reaches down and
>touches the earth.*

Don't worry, it's not so cold.

>*Beat.*

Please, Sonya, I – I worked in hospital in Moscow—

>*SONYA turns to leave but lingers. Beat.*

I know I'm not a good person, Sonya, but I love you, and
I won't hurt you.

>*Beat.*

(*gentle*) Come.

>*SONYA and PIOTR hold their pose. The VIOLINIST
>walks across the stage, playing sweetly at first, then
>making discordant, jarring sounds as he passes between
>the lovers. Time elapses. PIOTR is digging a small grave
>in the moonlight. We hear the sound of his shovel hitting*

> *the stage. SONYA is holding her shawl wrapped into the*
> *shape of a baby.*

SONYA   Why so big a grave, Piotr?

> *Beat.*

Doesn't need to be so big.

> *Beat.*

Just little.

> *Beat.*

Just a little piece of blanket.

> *PIOTR stops digging, crosses himself and walks away.*
> *SONYA stands over the grave and holds the baby over it.*
> *As she lets the baby fall, it transforms back into her*
> *shawl.*

(*To the audience.*) Okay, so problem of Sonya is…!

> *SONYA contemplates the audience.*

Ahn, yes, I see what you are thinking. You are thinking, here comes Russian part of the play. Well, is Russian play. Some laughing, and then misery!

> *Beat.*

Okay, so, is okay. Don't worry, problem of Sonya is solved. Maybe she's a little uncomfortable in the heart, and also between the legs, but love is shit like that, ahn ladies?

> *Beat.*

On walk home to flower shop, Sonya is feeling little better. She is thinking, next time she fall in love with Kulak's son, running lots of factory, not with gravedigger with wife in Moscow.

> *Beat.*

When Sonya go into flower shop, she take off her shoes and walk on tip of toes for not to make any noise. She get to little corner in back of shop where she sleep. She take off shawl and she take off skirt, and there is shop owner standing in doorway.

Beat.

Shop owner with look on face like she drink bad vodka and want to spit it out.

Beat.

Sonya say to her, "Hello, I'm sorry, I went for walk in cold to feel better. I was sick." Shop owner nod her head and smile, but not so nice a smile, and she say, "Ahn sick, that's what you call it? Did he make you feel better? That Moscow gravedigger? He digs graves all over Russia, I hear."

Beat.

"No, I told you I was sick!" But the shop owner say, "Where did you lie down with him, in the graveyard? Whose grave did you lie on? That little boy Dmitri, died of fever? Or Varya, good wife to butcher for twenty-three years?"

Beat.

"No, is not true!" But the shop owner say to Sonya, "You smell like corpse. Can't have that smell in my shop. Make the flowers die. Make the customers sick to their stomach." And she push Sonya out of the door.

Beat.

Winter is not so good a time to look for job, and in Vladekstov, gossip is like drinking vodka. How else to make the time go by? Soon, whole town know about the flower-shop girl and the gravedigger. The men are saying, "That Sonya. I wouldn't mind being gravedigger if such girls come to you." And the wives are saying, "Ahn yes, that Sonya, I always say she was trouble."

Beat.

Piotr? He leave back to his wife in Moscow on first train out of Vladekstov. And Sonya? She is shit out for work. Who will give job to no-good ex-mistress of gravedigger?

Beat.

She ask at factory, she ask at farm, but....

Beat.

Soon, Sonya leave Vladekstov and travel to nearby Smolensk. But even in Smolensk, with lots of shop, lots of factory, work is not so easy to find.

Beat.

Soon, Sonya's skirt is a little dirty, her hair is a little greasy, the skin fall away from the bone.

Beat.

Soon, she is selling flowers in the streets. In the streets, she is selling flowers....

Beat.

We all know what happens to flower-shop girls when they run out of rubles, yes? They learn that love have...

KOSTYA enters.

...market value.

(to KOSTYA) Mister, please, some flowers for you? Some flowers, mister?

KOSTYA   I remember you. *(He considers her.)* From Vladekstov! From the shop, by the graveyard, yes?

SONYA   Yes.

KOSTYA   *(trying to remember her name)* Sonya?

SONYA   Yes.

KOSTYA   Yes, that's right. Sonya, in the flower shop. So young and so beautiful.

SONYA   You are Kostya, the Kulak's son.

KOSTYA   That's right.

SONYA   Married to that no-good girl, Anya.

> *SONYA laughs, then puts her head down, embarrassed.*

KOSTYA   That's funny.

SONYA   I brought flowers to your house for the wedding.

KOSTYA   Tell me, Sonya. I hear you like graveyards. Do you also like factories?

> *SONYA pulls away.*

No, please, I'm sorry. Look, let me buy some flowers. They're very beautiful. Very beautiful flowers for sale.

> *Lights out on KOSTYA.*

SONYA   *(to audience)* Here is rich Kulak's son in Smolensk! Buying flowers from Sonya in Smolensk, can you believe? Can you believe such luck of this?!

> *Beat.*

He have wife, yes, he have wife, but who don't have wife, ahn, ladies?

> *SONYA sings the Russian song, flirting with KOSTYA. SONYA begins to sing and dance for him as he enters.*

Smee-yom-sya, smee-yom-sya,
Cheerez pol-ya,
Cheerez pol-ya, ha ha ha,
Mee smee-yom-sya.

KOSTYA   I like this song.

> *SONYA sits on KOSTYA's lap.*

SONYA   *(flirting)* Tell me. Are all men cold in their wives' beds?

KOSTYA   *(laughs)* Yes. You still think of him? Your Moscow gravedigger.

SONYA   No.

KOSTYA   No?

SONYA   No gravedigger, please, big mistake. What can he do
for you? Ahn? What? Maybe dig grave for you when you
are dead?!

> *KOSTYA laughs.*

Did you bring me here to laugh at me?

KOSTYA   No.

SONYA   No, I didn't think so.

> *They kiss. As KOSTYA puts his hand up SONYA's
> skirt, the lights fade out on KOSTYA.*

(to audience) Okay! So! We all understand the picture here.

> *Beat.*

The Kulak's son, he keep Sonya in little room in hotel. He
come to see her twice, three times, sometime four times
a week. Soon people of Smolensk hear about the Kulak's
son and the ex-flower-shop girl. But this time, no one say
anything. Because the Kulak's son? He is not just in bed
with Sonya. He is also in bed with secret police, with
Soviet bureaucrat. And who knows, maybe with Stalin
himself.

> *Lights up on KOSTYA, in the hotel room.*

KOSTYA   I like this Stalin. Either you want new Russia, or you
don't want new Russia. And Stalin? He want new Russia.

SONYA   Just like you, Kostya.

> *KOSTYA kisses her hand.*

KOSTYA   Sonya, Sonya! My little shop girl.

SONYA   Kostya. Please.

KOSTYA   There are lots of girls like you, Sonya, factories full of
them. But I don't know why – why I...!

> *Beat.*

I could pick any girl. But—

SONYA   You will be late for your wife, Kostya. She will be
angry.

KOSTYA   I don't care! I don't care about my wife!

SONYA   You will care when she's yelling at you!

KOSTYA   No I won't, I won't listen, I will think of you in this little room, looking like flower!

> *SONYA and KOSTYA laugh, and he spins her around and admires her. The lights fade on him as he exits. SONYA stops laughing and contemplates the audience.*

SONYA   *(to audience)* Not so simple what to think of this Kulak's son. Some of you are thinking Kostya is good enough man, lots of factories, lots of rubles. Sonya is okay, is looked after. So why are you still sitting here? Why is play still going?

> *Beat.*

But some of you are having more romantic thought. Ahn? Ladies!?

> *Beat.*

Sonya try not to think about Piotr. She try not to think about Piotr when Kostya come to see her, when Kostya look at her, when he put his arms around her.

> *PIOTR enters as SONYA says the above. He puts his arms around her, holds her, kisses her. SONYA smiles. The lights flicker. Now it's KOSTYA holding her.*

KOSTYA   *(sexual)* Sonya, Sonya!

SONYA   Kostya, Kostya, will you—

KOSTYA   *(sexual)* What?

SONYA   —bring me… glass of vodka?

> *KOSTYA stops short, looks at her, exits.*

(to audience) For long time, Sonya live in hotel in Smolensk, she keep her mouth shut, and she hold down misery. She hold down misery using lots of vodka. But problem with vodka? It make you forget, but it also give you courage.

> *Lights up on KOSTYA.*

KOSTYA   I am meeting with police. They are waiting for me, Sonya, I can't fight with you right now.

SONYA   So don't fight with me.

KOSTYA   Come Sonya, please, don't be crazy. My wife is crazy, I don't need more crazy, okay?

> *Beat.*

> *(indulging her)* Where would you go?

SONYA   I don't know. Moscow?

KOSTYA   Moscow. I don't understand. Why don't you love me? What? You love gravedigger but you don't love me? Why not?

> *Beat.*

> Why not?

SONYA   Look after your wife!

KOSTYA   No, tell me, why don't you love me, Sonya?

SONYA   I don't know! I try, but—

KOSTYA   Who are you not to love me? Flower-shop girl with bad history. Opening your legs to gravediggers and Soviet traitors.

SONYA   That's right, I'm just ex-flower-shop girl with shit luck and bad history, so why not let me go? Lots of other girls!

> *KOSTYA holds SONYA. She struggles.*

KOSTYA   Please, Sonya, I love you, don't be crazy.

> *SONYA hits him and pushes him away. KOSTYA stumbles. He steadies himself. KOSTYA looks at her, considers, seems to make a decision, exits.*

SONYA   *(to audience)* What can I tell to you? Sonya is stupid girl, yes? Stupid Russian girl, lots of girls like Sonya, factories full of them.

> *Beat.*

So. Vodka is not so strong now, and Sonya is not so sure anymore what her big idea was when she wanted to go to Moscow. But, as Kostya leave her hotel room, as she think about long train to Moscow, she feel like light is shining on her. She pack her bag, she put on her shawl, she open the door and there is police standing in doorway.

Beat.

Police with look on their faces like they eat bad pork and want to spit it out.

Beat.

"Hello," Sonya say to police, "I am just leaving for Moscow. Did Kostya send you for something?" The police nod their heads, and they smile to each other, and they say to her, "You want to go to Moscow, Sonya? Is no problem, let us take you. Is maybe not so comfortable in Moscow as here in Smolensk, but don't worry, we will look after you."

Beat.

"No, is okay," Sonya say to the police, "I don't want you to take me. Tell Kostya I don't want to go anymore. Tell him I want to stay in Smolensk." The police laugh when they hear this, and they say, "What? You don't like Moscow so much anymore? Well then, what about Siberia?"

Beat.

"No, wait. Please, Kostya is not happy with me now, but, if you let me speak with him, he will change back his mind. Please, please let me speak to him. Let me speak to him!"

Beat.

Sonya travel to Moscow in cattle cart of train.

Beat.

Sonya travel for three days, alone with police, in cattle cart of train.

We hear PIOTR, off, singing the Russian song.

In Moscow prison, Sonya start to go a little crazy.

Beat.

Maybe is because of the police interrogations. Maybe is because they tell her to say she is enemy of people so they can send her to work camp, maybe because they don't give for her anything to eat, because they pull out her fingernails one by one and leave her standing in cold water for many hours, maybe because she is turning into just blood and bones, sometime Sonya think she can hear Piotr singing.

SONYA listens to the singing.

Singing like he used to sing to her in Vladekstov grave-yard.

Beat.

(*calling*) Piotr?

The singing and the violin cut out. SONYA listens for a moment and then looks away. After a moment, the singing starts again.

Sonya is going a little crazy.

Beat. PIOTR steps into the light.

PIOTR   Sonya?

SONYA   Piotr?

PIOTR   Sonya.

SONYA   Piotr. You are police now?

PIOTR   No. I am working in graveyard, back of prison.

PIOTR stares at her. SONYA tries to straighten her skirt.

SONYA   I not looking like you remember?

PIOTR   No, Sonya you look.... You need bread, I think I have.

PIOTR reaches into his pocket.

SONYA   How is wife? She is here in Moscow, yes?

PIOTR   No.

SONYA   No?

PIOTR   No. She... died. Not long after I left Vladekstov.

Beat.

SONYA   Wife died?

PIOTR   Yes.

SONYA   And you didn't come back? You didn't come back to Vladekstov and look for me? Why not? Why didn't you come. Why wouldn't you come back, Piotr?

PIOTR   Because! Because of Kulak. Kulak in Smolensk, yes? You were happy? You were looked after?

SONYA   No!

PIOTR   You were not happy?

SONYA   No! How could I be happy? I loved you! I loved you, Piotr.

PIOTR   Sonya, I loved you too. I loved you and I left you there. I left you and life was difficult and full of misery, and I loved you, I don't know why I—

PIOTR reacts to footsteps he hears, off. He steps back and looks down the corridor.

SONYA   Is police coming?

Beat.

Piotr? Is police?

PIOTR steps toward her.

PIOTR   *(low)* Sonya, take bread. Don't show.

PIOTR hands her the bread, looks behind him and then quickly turns away and exits.

SONYA   *(calling after him)* Is police? Piotr!

Beat.

(to audience) Sonya is thinking, the bread! The bread Piotr give to her! The police will see and will want to know where is from, and what will she say? Not from Piotr. She can't say from Piotr, or they will…

> *Beat.*

Sonya know what will happen to Piotr if she tell them that he…

> *Beat.*

She have to hide the bread, so they can't find, the police who look everywhere. Is big piece, where to hide? She stuff into mouth but is too big. She can't put in shoe, they look in shoe, she can't put in skirt, they look in skirt. Can't put in stocking, they look in stocking. Where to hide piece of bread, I ask myself this. I am looking for answer.

> *SONYA reaches between her skirts and all the way up, and with a little jerk, she pulls out a piece of bread. She holds it out. She picks a hair off of it.*

Stupid place to put bread.

> *Beat.*

Stupid Sonya.

> *Beat.*

Doesn't think of infection.

> *Beat.*

Infection from bread, can you believe?

> *Beat.*

For two weeks Sonya is in prison hospital ward, slowly turning black.

> *PIOTR starts digging her grave, off. SONYA crumbles the bread in her hand. She contemplates the audience.*

Okay. So. Let me level to you. This is my shit Russian love story. Stupid, stupid Sonya, I am embarrass to myself. I fall in love with Piotr, and that's my whole life gone for shit.

PIOTR continues digging, off.

I lose flower-shop job for Piotr, Kostya send police for me for Piotr, and now, in Moscow prison, I kill myself for Piotr. This is love for you!

Beat.

Ladies, I have to tell you, you won't like to hear, but love is like Russia. There are some beautiful pieces, but mostly it's shit. Ahn, ladies? You were thinking is beautiful, my story? The gravedigger and the flower-shop girl, is like poetry, yes?

Beat.

Well! Let me tell to you. Love is—!

PIOTR enters and puts his arms around SONYA. She feels his warmth. She is terribly, terribly happy.

The VIOLINIST stops playing abruptly. SONYA is dead in PIOTR's arms. As PIOTR lays SONYA in the grave, the lights fade out.

Music by Claire Jenkins with Tom Howell.

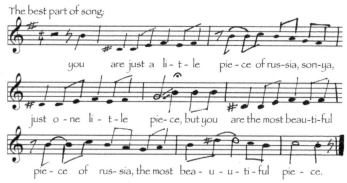

Gravedigger's Song:
pizzicato

Kostya's Theme:

MUSIC NOT3S

These four tunes are the basic musical themes throughout the play. The "Song Piotr is always singing" is the main theme that keeps reappearing, especially the first phrase. The tunes can be subverted, built on, broken up or repeated, whatever best suits the production. The musician is in a kind of dialogue with the story and so the music is very much interwoven. The phrases don't necessarily have to be completed every time they are started. The singing parts are there for the actors to act through and can be played with in order to best suit the action.

"The Gravedigger's Song" appears for the first time when Sonya introduces us to Piotr in the graveyard. "Kostya's Theme" appears with Sonja's arrival in Smolensk.

The musician also creates sound effects. For instance, Sonya's journey in the "cattle cart of train" may be accompanied by playing col legno, bouncing the back of the bow on the strings. This creates an effective space for the scene.

ESSAY

Essay premiered at the SummerWorks Theatre Festival (an Absit Omen Theatre production) in Toronto on August 5th, 2005, with the following company:

JEFFREY	Jordan Pettle
PIXIE	Claire Jenkins
PROF. GALBRAITH	Richard Greenblatt

Director: Michael Rubenfeld
Assistant Director: Caleb Yong

Essay won the 2005 Contra Guys Award for Best New Script
at the SummerWorks Theatre Festival.

Essay was later produced at Factory Theatre in Toronto as part of a double bill with *The Russian Play* in January of 2008, with the following company:

JEFFREY	Jordan Pettle
PIXIE	Claire Jenkins
PROF. GALBRAITH	Richard Greenblatt

Director: Michael Rubenfeld
Set & Costume Design: Camellia Koo
Lighting Design: Kimberly Purtell
Sound Design: Thomas Ryder Payne
Assistant Set & Costume Design: Anna Treusch
Stage Manager: Joanna Barrotta
Assistant Stage Manager: Alexandra Stephanoff

CHARACTERS

JEFFREY: thirty
PIXIE: eighteen
PROFESSOR GALBRAITH: early sixties

ESSAY

SCENE ONE

A small office on campus. An open laptop sits on a desk amidst piles of papers, files and books. The greenish hue of fluorescent lighting fills the room. Lights up on JEFFREY, behind the desk, and PIXIE, in front of it.

JEFFREY   Just, uh, please take a seat while I finish this paragraph and then I'll leave off.

PIXIE   Am I early…? Or…?

JEFFREY   No, no, just finishing up, just finishing up.

JEFFREY closes his laptop.

Now. Essay proposal, is that right? Essay due on the eighteenth?

PIXIE   Thank you for letting me come and—

JEFFREY   No, please. Just remind me. I rejected your proposal, is that…?

PIXIE   Uh, yes, you did, but—

JEFFREY   Right. Good. Well, my notes are vague sometimes, and my handwriting is very bad, so before you raze the field, we might as well take a closer look at it.

PIXIE   *(getting out her essay proposal)* Okay, great, um, well what I wanted to—

JEFFREY   It's usually just a question of coming up with an alteration that will render it—

PIXIE   —um, okay—

JEFFREY   —more precise, more scholarly.

PIXIE   Okay. That's what I wanted to talk to you about.

JEFFREY   Good. Yes. Let's talk!

PIXIE   Your objections, because I – I think I can make an argument for this essay proposal.

JEFFREY   This one?

PIXIE   Yeah.

JEFFREY   This essay proposal?

PIXIE   Yes?

> *Beat.*

JEFFREY   Ah. I see. You've come to contest.

PIXIE   Or at least I just wanted to—

JEFFREY   To make your case, is that it?

PIXIE   I – I just think that – that it's possible – that it's possible to argue, I mean if the problem is just sourcing.

JEFFREY   Let me take a look at it, can I?

> *PIXIE hands him the essay proposal.*

Let's just see what we've got here before we… *(laughs)* …have it out.

> *Beat.*

PIXIE   *(waiting, shifting)* If – if you read the notes you made…

> *JEFFREY holds out his hand to indicate to PIXIE that she should give him a minute to finish reading.*

> *Beat.*

JEFFREY   *(scanning)* Elizabeth Farnese. Strategies of, important contributions to. Summary, summary, more summary. Look. What you've got here is very interesting. A very interesting historical figure—

PIXIE   Yeah, well I thought—

JEFFREY   —who no doubt deserves more…. An argument could be made that this is an oversight. The historical record has failed to illuminate this neglected but highly engaging corner of European history.

PIXIE   Unhunh, well—

JEFFREY   Hoards of insensitive historians have obscured a very important character, as it were.

PIXIE   Yeah, well—

JEFFREY   And she is worthy, entitled to, a second glance, now, in our modern era. However, that said—

PIXIE   Unhunh.

JEFFREY   —that said, I'm not sure that for the purposes of this first year course it's – it's—if there would be enough material to support a ten-page essay on the topic.

PIXIE   Yeah, but—

JEFFREY   Ten pages. You'll need more than a cursory—

PIXIE   Yeah.

JEFFREY   —more than a brief mention in a larger—

PIXIE   Yeah, I have. I have plenty of material. And also, there's one listed at the bottom of the supplementary readings, on page twenty-one.

JEFFREY   One what?

PIXIE   An article on her.

    Beat.

JEFFREY   That's very possible, all right.

PIXIE   And I found ample sources in the stacks.

JEFFREY   That's very possible.

PIXIE   And the article was on the list—

JEFFREY   Right, right I see the—now we're getting to the bottom of the—

PIXIE   —and so—

JEFFREY   This is progress!

PIXIE   And so, I thought—

JEFFREY   You thought it was on the list, it must be—

PIXIE   Yeah.

JEFFREY   And I want to stress that your idea is not invalid, by any means, all right?

PIXIE   Unhunh.

JEFFREY   At least not in general terms, all right?

PIXIE   Unhunh?

> *Beat.*

JEFFREY   I'm not the – I don't want to be the big bad—

PIXIE   Yeah?

JEFFREY   —the big bad—

PIXIE   Yeah?

JEFFREY   Is that…? Is it Pixie? Is that your…?

PIXIE   Yeah. Pixie.

JEFFREY   Look, Pixie—

PIXIE   Yeah?

JEFFREY   I understand you feel very passionately about this. Here you are in my office, overflowing with passion… *(laughs)* …

> *PIXIE shifts away from JEFFREY.*

No, no, what I mean is you've made the effort to come here, to defend your proposal to me, the topic you've chosen indicates that you're trying to avoid the banal and revitalize history, as it were, and so—

PIXIE   Yeah?

JEFFREY   I want to stress that I appreciate your passion.

> *Beat.*

PIXIE   But—

JEFFREY   Your topic is frankly…. You see, this is a history course that—

PIXIE   And this is history.

JEFFREY   Yes, yes it's history, but Pixie, this course deals with war and statecraft. In the eighteenth and early nineteenth century.

PIXIE   Yeah?

JEFFREY   Eighteenth and early nineteenth century. Now I'm not saying that women haven't, in more recent times, made very valuable contributions to war efforts. But, in the eighteenth century, women didn't yet—

PIXIE   —unhuhn—

JEFFREY   —possess the freedom of movement, the – the wherewithal to—

PIXIE   —unhuhn—

JEFFREY   —and so women couldn't as yet be classified as "military leaders," per se.

PIXIE   Okay, but—

JEFFREY   And—just a minute—and that is why I can't allow you to write a paper on a woman who, while she may be very compelling from a social history perspective—

PIXIE   Yeah, but she—

JEFFREY   —is not an appropriate subject given the requirements of this particular writing assignment. Now I commend you for finding source material. Good work there! But the thing is you're simply not on topic.

> *JEFFREY hands back PIXIE's essay proposal.*

If you need to hear this from a higher source, by all means, take it up with the professor, he is the final word—

PIXIE   No, it's fine, I'm just – I don't know, a little—

JEFFREY   Disappointed, I see that.

PIXIE   No, I'm confused.

JEFFREY   Yes. Confused, disappointed, and believe me, I understand. European history is a... bewildering series of men who prance about, waging war, and making a nuisance of themselves. And so, you light on Elizabeth Farnese because you'd like to champion her, establish her worth, she is one of the unacknowledged greats of history, and that's a very understandable response given the material—

PIXIE   Wait.

JEFFREY   —the time period—

PIXIE   You—wait—you think I picked her because she's a girl? You think I picked Elizabeth Farnese because she's a girl.

> *Beat.*

JEFFREY   Well, what I was suggesting wasn't quite so simplistic—

PIXIE   I didn't. I really – I'm not a feminist. It said war and strategy and she was a great strategist, really, if you read the material I found.

JEFFREY   I – Pixie, I'm sure she was, but—

PIXIE   She was.

JEFFREY   I'm sure she was, but—

PIXIE   She was. She was a great strategist, she played everyone. The French, the Austrians—

JEFFREY   Yes, Pixie, that's the history.

PIXIE   Well, that's why I picked her. 'Cause I thought that was on topic.

JEFFREY   I – let's back up here for a moment—

PIXIE   I thought I was on topic.

JEFFREY   Pixie, let's – please, let's back up for a moment—

PIXIE   If I'm not on topic, then—

JEFFREY   Pixie! Please. I want to – we must address a statement you made a moment ago. Did I, or am I mistaken, hear you say you're not a feminist?

PIXIE   No, I'm not, I was just doing the assignment.

JEFFREY   Yes, yes, but—

PIXIE   I thought it was just a question of sources. That's what you wrote on my sheet, that's why I came here.

JEFFREY   Yes, but Pixie. Feminism—

PIXIE   I'm not a feminist.

JEFFREY   But you… *(laughs uncomfortably)* …I don't think you—

PIXIE   I'm not. I took this course. I wanted to take the history of war, I didn't take a women's studies course—

JEFFREY   —but—

PIXIE   —I took this course.

JEFFREY   But, Pixie, women's studies is a very valuable body of knowledge, and you are a feminist.

PIXIE   No I'm not.

JEFFREY   Yes you…! Perhaps you don't realize—

PIXIE   I'm not a feminist—

JEFFREY   —because the very fact that you're standing here, before me, in this institution – a hundred years ago, fifty, that would not have been possible, and you would not have received adequate education to be able to argue to me that Elizabeth Farnese is a military leader—

PIXIE   No, this is the point. I didn't pick her because she's a girl.

JEFFREY   But Pixie—

PIXIE   I didn't go looking for some girl so I could pick her, so I could make some big point to you to vindicate women or whatever you're thinking—

JEFFREY   Why did you pick her, then?

         Beat.

    Why pick her?

         Beat.

PIXIE   Okay. Fine. I picked a girl. But the point I was trying to make about not being a feminist was—

JEFFREY   You are a feminist.

PIXIE   No I'm not.

JEFFREY   Yes you...! Pixie, look—

PIXIE   I'm not.

JEFFREY   Look. Take you and I, you and I, Pixie. You believe
yourself to be equal to me, don't you?

PIXIE   I'm your student.

JEFFREY   Yes, but, aside from our status as – as – I'm a bad
example. Take any of your fellow students, the male
members of your classes, you believe yourself to be equal
to them, don't you?

> *Beat.*

That's feminism. That is feminism. And so you are, by
definition—

PIXIE   Fine. Fine. I'm a feminist.

JEFFREY   Now, all right—

PIXIE   I'm a fucking feminist.

JEFFREY   All right. Let's not – let's please—

PIXIE   All I was trying to say was I thought Elizabeth Farnese
was really effective and interesting, but I don't care,
okay? I'll write on Napoleon.

JEFFREY   Yes, all right.

PIXIE   I'll write on Napoleon like everyone else.

JEFFREY   Pixie. Please, just slow down. Let's not raise our
voices please.

> *Beat.*

PIXIE   *(more confused than sorry)* Sorry.

JEFFREY   That's all right.

> *Beat.*

Napoleon would be a highly appropriate choice, in the
context of this...

PIXIE has walked out.

Pixie, where are you going?

JEFFREY walks after her.

Can you – can we please finish our...?

Beat.

Pixie?

PIXIE is gone. JEFFREY shakes his head, and goes back over his desk. He crosses off his meeting with PIXIE in his date book. Lights out.

SCENE TWO

JEFFREY's office, a week and a half later. There is a pile of essays on his desk. JEFFREY is marking. PROFESSOR GALBRAITH enters and looks at the office.

GALBRAITH   This is a dismal little office, Jeffrey.

JEFFREY   *(standing)* Professor Galbraith!

GALBRAITH   I haven't been down here since, well, the seventies, and I don't think it's changed.

JEFFREY   Thank you for... stopping by.

GALBRAITH   Who are you sharing it with, some social science...?

JEFFREY   She's, yes, an anthropology Ph.D., but she's on a very different schedule, opposite hours—

GALBRAITH   Good.

JEFFREY   It's worked out well. I barely ever see her.

Beat.

And I keep meaning to say thank you for finding me / this office—

GALBRAITH   So what's the matter, Jeffrey? Hm? Your email, your phone call? I'm sorry I've been unresponsive, the conference—

JEFFREY   Yes, I know, the timing—

GALBRAITH   I agreed to moderate a couple of panels, deliver a keynote, and suddenly when the coffee machine breaks down, they all come to me.

JEFFREY   Yes, I can see how that / would happen.

GALBRAITH   This is the downside of heading the department. There are upsides! There are upsides!

JEFFREY   I'm sure there are.

> *Beat.*

So, / Professor—

GALBRAITH   So what is it, Jeffrey? Hm? You need to consult? You need to be supervised? Someone to hold your hand?

JEFFREY   Well—

GALBRAITH   It's difficult, this juncture in the dissertation-writing process. The tunnel, they call it.

JEFFREY   Uh, no—

GALBRAITH   Which is apt because you're pretty much hunting down your own asshole at this point, excuse the…. Because, once the research is done and you're writing—

JEFFREY   Yes, no, I—

GALBRAITH   —there it is, looming on the horizon, your own anus. That's what a Ph.D. is. An heroic-apocalyptic confrontation with the self.

JEFFREY   Professor, that's very… funny, and sometimes it does feel as though I'm peering into my own… but no, it's not my dissertation.

GALBRAITH   Dissertation is going well, is it?

JEFFREY   Yes, it's going, but I've been trying to grade the essays for History 103?

> *GALBRAITH picks up a pile of essays.*

GALBRAITH   This them?

JEFFREY   Yes, and what I need to ask you is—

GALBRAITH   Lots of little comments. Good point. This is awkward.

JEFFREY   *(laughs)* Yes.

GALBRAITH   Where's your thesis?

JEFFREY   Yes… *(laughs)* …and, uh, Professor, what I wanted to ask you is—

GALBRAITH   I haven't seen you at the conference, by the way.

>   *Beat.*

JEFFREY   No. I haven't been attending. I've been so intent on getting through these—

GALBRAITH   I chaired what turned out to be a very energetic panel on interpretations of Napoleonic law.

JEFFREY   Well, I'm sorry I missed it.

GALBRAITH   Also a lecture on problems of coalition warfare. Quite compelling. A Chicago University professor, Sheila Newbery. Right up your alley, research wise. I hope you weren't grading undergraduate essays rather than attending the conference?

JEFFREY   I – well – I—

GALBRAITH   I hope you were at least chasing – or – what's the euphemism these days for female companionship? The conference falls a little short there. One look at the participants and…. *(laughs)* Don't expect to find love in the history department, Jeffrey.

JEFFREY   I… won't hold my breath. *(trying to joke)* Perhaps the English department.

GALBRAITH   There's a good hunting ground. The English department!

>   *PROFESSOR GALBRAITH and JEFFREY share
>   a laugh. Beat.*

JEFFREY   Professor, I wanted to ask you—

GALBRAITH   Oh, right, yes, ask me the—

JEFFREY   A student of mine, an essay—

GALBRAITH   Right.

> *JEFFREY begins looking through the pile for PIXIE's essay.*

JEFFREY   I'm trying to grade this one paper, but it's very difficult. I rejected this student's essay proposal when she submitted it two weeks ago. We discussed it, I thought she'd resolved to write on a more appropriate topic, but, as it turns out, she hasn't. She's written on the original.

GALBRAITH   Ah.

JEFFREY   And, yes, and now I'm not sure whether to fail her, or what's the procedure? I told her to come by my office this afternoon, thinking I'd have a chance to confer with you first—

> *JEFFREY finds the essay and hands it to PROFESSOR GALBRAITH.*

The title should give you a good sense of the type of—

GALBRAITH   Cock-up?

JEFFREY   Yes.

> *Beat. PROFESSOR GALBRAITH and JEFFREY look at the title.*

GALBRAITH   Hmmm, yes! Quite the—

JEFFREY   You see the…

> *Beat.*

GALBRAITH   *(reading)* Elizabeth Farnese and Napoleon Bonaparte: A Critical Comparison of their Wartime Strategies.

JEFFREY   You see the difficulty. And, for grading, it reads like an English paper, all conjecture and—

GALBRAITH   Yes.

> *Beat.*

JEFFREY   The sources are fine, but—

GALBRAITH   Yes.

> *Beat.*

> Yes, this certainly isn't what I discussed with her. I didn't approve a comparison. Although, I suppose she was trying to appease you and write on her topic. Servant of two masters.

> *PROFESSOR GALBRAITH looks through the essay.*

JEFFREY   I'm… sorry. I'm sorry, Professor. You – did she—

GALBRAITH   Didn't I tell you, Jeffrey? This girl came to see me a week, a week and a half ago, asked if she could write on Elizabeth Farnese, Philip the fifth's second wife?

JEFFREY   *(to confirm that he knows who she is)* Yes.

GALBRAITH   How Elizabeth Farnese is a military leader… *(laughs)* …I'm interested to know.

> *PROFESSOR GALBRAITH flips through the essay.*

JEFFREY   Yes, but, she's not. I'm sorry, she's not, at least not considered to be—

GALBRAITH   Elizabeth Farnese?

JEFFREY   She's not generally considered to be a military leader—

GALBRAITH   No, no, of course not. But, she seemed…. This girl – the girl…?

JEFFREY   Pixie Findley?

GALBRAITH   She seemed very – I'm probably looking for attractive, but let's say determined for the sake of decorum. I thought, why not let her have a go, she's likely going to argue something preposterous. Has she?

JEFFREY   I – I don't know.

GALBRAITH   I was hoping for something a little risqué, at least euphemistically, as in Elizabeth Farnese's victories were won not on the battlefield but in the bedroom, or

Frederick the Great favoured the oblique attack while Elizabeth perfected the horizontal one, something to that effect.

PROFESSOR GALBRAITH reads through the essay.

JEFFREY   But the guidelines for this essay were very specific—

GALBRAITH   I let the leash out a little.

Beat.

JEFFREY   I – yes – I can see why you might. I hesitated, uh, briefly before I rejected her proposal. It's sensitive, of course, and highly charged, but the reason why I ultimately did turn her down was—

GALBRAITH   *(referring to PIXIE's essay)* This is quite good, this opening.

Beat.

JEFFREY   The reason, Professor, why I didn't allow Pixie to write on Elizabeth Farnese is that I felt fairly certain that, given the parameters of the assignment that you set, military leader, it would result in her producing a very weak essay.

Beat.

And she has produced a very weak essay. Professor.

GALBRAITH   Ah, now, here we have it! *(reading from PIXIE's essay)* "While Napoleon engaged in warfare to resolve international strife," very nice, "Elizabeth relied on her feminine wiles."

JEFFREY   Professor.

GALBRAITH   Very nice phrasing. Wiles. Where do you suppose her wiles were located?

JEFFREY   Look, I—

GALBRAITH   Adjacent to her thighs, presumably.

JEFFREY   I – Professor – this is a student's essay!

GALBRAITH stops reading PIXIE's essay and looks at JEFFREY.

I realize some of it's laughable, but…

    Beat.

I'm sorry, I'm just a little surprised you allowed a student to write on Elizabeth Farnese.

GALBRAITH   What are you concerned about, Jeffrey? Her grade?

JEFFREY   Well, yes, her grade, but also—

GALBRAITH   Pass her, write a few comments on it. Good effort. Fails to convince.

JEFFREY   I suppose I can do that. This essay certainly doesn't deserve a passing grade. I don't feel all that comfortable with—

GALBRAITH   Jeffrey—

JEFFREY   —arbitrarily assigning it one.

    Beat.

GALBRAITH   B minus.

    Beat.

JEFFREY   No – you – no, the point is, I'm forced to arbitrarily assign her a grade because she was allowed to write on a, I think, inappropriate… B minus. That's at least a firm hold on the material. Look, I – I really don't like being put in this position at all, I feel very—

GALBRAITH   Jeffrey.

JEFFREY   B minus? Based on what criteria?

GALBRAITH   Well, no doubt she learned something while writing it.

JEFFREY   She learned. She learned something. That's your criterion?

GALBRAITH   You don't like my criterion?

JEFFREY   This is a very unconvincing essay!

GALBRAITH   How bad can it be?

JEFFREY   It's a terrible essay! It's ridiculous.

GALBRAITH   Jeffrey.

JEFFREY   A short story would be more convincing. A finger-painting!

GALBRAITH   Oh, for Christ's sake, Jeffrey, she wrote a bad essay! The girl is seventeen. Eighteen. Let her go skip off and neck in the quad.

>   *Beat.*

JEFFREY   Neck in the…!

GALBRAITH   Or what do they say, make out?

>   *Beat.*

JEFFREY   Professor, this is the student who argued that Elizabeth Farnese is a military leader, and now you're trivializing—

GALBRAITH   All right—

JEFFREY   —and – and ridiculing her very earnest attempt—

GALBRAITH   All right!

JEFFREY   —to include women in the history of—

GALBRAITH   Yes, I know, Jeffrey, because I'm the one who let her. I approved her essay topic. I said yes. Write on Elizabeth Farnese. Prove she's on par with Nelson, Napoleon. Set us all straight, us men.

>   *Beat.*

>   *(smiling)* We have to let the girls have their day, Jeffrey.

>   *Beat.*

JEFFREY   We have to… let the girls…?

>   *Beat.*

>   I'm sorry?

GALBRAITH   In my experience, it's best to just let them, well, have their day.

>   *Beat.*

JEFFREY   What do you mean?

GALBRAITH   It may make for weak scholarship, but I think it's best to allow for it, at the moment, despite its weaknesses.

> *Beat.*

JEFFREY   I – I'm sorry. What – what makes for weak scholarship?

GALBRAITH   There's a great deal of so-called research in circulation these days that's entirely based on resentment.

JEFFREY   What are you talking about?

GALBRAITH   Gendered revisionism, Jeffrey. Biographies of Napoleon's lover, James Joyce's wife, the unsung women of history, herstory, all very fashionable, but at a certain point... *(laughs)* ...it fails to convince.

> *Beat.*

JEFFREY   It – it fails to... are you joking? Professor?

GALBRAITH   You said it yourself. Pixie's essay is a failure. Why? Because Elizabeth Farnese is, at best, a second-rate figure who cannot yield any important historical insight.

JEFFREY   Yes, perhaps in the context of this assignment—

GALBRAITH   And the result, an unscholarly, as you said, paper—

JEFFREY   But not as a general—

GALBRAITH   That you deemed weak—

JEFFREY   I – I wouldn't make that kind of a sweeping—

GALBRAITH   That you rejected—

JEFFREY   Yes! I – yes – I rejected her essay proposal, not the whole field of inquiry!

> *Beat.*

GALBRAITH   All right, Jeffrey, what is history? What is it?

> *Beat.*

JEFFREY   What is... history?

GALBRAITH   Too broad? What isn't history?

>   *Beat.*

JEFFREY   What is not—

GALBRAITH   What can we say is not history?

>   *Beat.*

>   Seventeenth, eighteenth century. What are men doing?

>   *Beat.*

>   Revolutionizing warfare. And what are women doing?

JEFFREY   Well, they're—

GALBRAITH   Curling their hair, boiling potatoes, et cetera, et cetera. They are not central to the major events. They are—it's unfortunate, it's unlikeable—marginal to them. If we want to include women, we have to reorient history to the mundane, and frankly—

JEFFREY   —uh, Professor—

GALBRAITH   —frankly—

JEFFREY   —Professor—

GALBRAITH   —then it's no longer history, is it? It's sociology, anthropology, women's studies-ology.

>   *Beat.*

JEFFREY   Look, Professor, that is all… very controversial and I—

GALBRAITH   What?

JEFFREY   I – I—

GALBRAITH   What?

JEFFREY   —disagree. I think we should be privileging a female discourse, given how excluded and sidelined—

GALBRAITH   So Elizabeth Farnese is a military leader.

JEFFREY   No, that's not – that's a bad example.

GALBRAITH   Which is it?

JEFFREY   I don't think it's an either-or—

GALBRAITH   So she is?

JEFFREY   Well, one could argue, I mean, as it stands, no.

GALBRAITH   So she isn't.

JEFFREY   No – she – I just – no, I don't think it's that simple. Because—

GALBRAITH   Jeffrey.

JEFFREY   No! Because one could argue, one could radically redefine the term military leader—

GALBRAITH   Yes, and one could write an essay about how Napoleon's horse influenced his decisions. If a horse came to you and asked if it could write that essay, you would probably say, let the horse have its day. Call it horsestory. And it may be true, to a certain extent, that Napoleon's horse did influence his decisions, but who really gives a damn?

   Beat.

JEFFREY   Professor, I'm sorry, are you actually not joking? Because I – I can't believe I'm hearing this.

GALBRAITH   Jeffrey, relax, all right?

JEFFREY   I can't believe you just said horsestory.

GALBRAITH   Jeffrey.

JEFFREY   Horsestory? Professor? Horsestory? That's a very pejorative, uh, derisive, misogynist—

GALBRAITH   Misogynist?

JEFFREY   I, yes, I think, misogynist—

GALBRAITH   All right, all right, relax, I'm... what? Toying with your liberal sensibilities? I'm not rejecting all revisionism, per se. However, one gets tired, worn down. The relentless onslaught of victimology. The history department's awash in it. We're being strangled to death by cultural studies. They've got their own fucking department, why do they want mine? What is wrong with Napoleon? Personally, I love the guy. You love the guy!

> *Beat.*

JEFFREY   Well, yes, but—

GALBRAITH   That's history, Jeffrey. That's history. A love affair with Napoleon.

JEFFREY   I – no, you see – no – I don't agree.

> *Beat.*

I disagree!

GALBRAITH   You're researching Napoleon—

JEFFREY   Yes, fine, I am, but I don't think Napoleon Bonaparte is the only valid…! I think this whole argument only highlights the fact that we've constructed a false notion of history as male, as centred on male events, male figures, in which case, we should be trying to update, and redress—

GALBRAITH   —yes, fine—

JEFFREY   —to try and right the balance.

GALBRAITH   Yes. You're right.

JEFFREY   And broaden the scope of…

> *Beat.*

I'm right.

GALBRAITH   Yes, I agree. I agree with you, as in Pixie's case. Pixie got to write her essay. Write on a female figure, have her say—

JEFFREY   No, but, no—

GALBRAITH   Right the balance, redress the what-have-you—

JEFFREY   But, no – that's not – no – you think her say has no merit.

> *Beat.*

You think it's merit-less.

GALBRAITH   So do you.

JEFFREY   But, no, look, that's patronizing.

GALBRAITH   No Jeffrey.

JEFFREY   That's – yes it is. You're humouring her, you're cynically appeasing her—

GALBRAITH   Pixie is happy.

> *Beat.*

JEFFREY   That's…! You're patronizing her!

GALBRAITH   I am allowing her to have her say.

JEFFREY   You don't value her say!

GALBRAITH   She can't tell the difference. If she can't tell the difference, then—

JEFFREY   What? Then it's not patronizing?

GALBRAITH   Then, no, it's not patronizing, largely because she doesn't feel patronized.

JEFFREY   Yes, but that's only because—

GALBRAITH   Or are you claiming to be better qualified to determine what's patronizing for Pixie than Pixie is herself?

JEFFREY   No, no I'm not. Except, yes, at this moment, yes, I'm the one who's—

GALBRAITH   What?

JEFFREY   Here! Listening to – privy to—

GALBRAITH   What?

JEFFREY   To… your—

GALBRAITH   What? Jeffrey?

JEFFREY   —sexism!

> *Long beat.*

GALBRAITH   Hm.

Beat.

Do you think you might be a little worn down?

JEFFREY   Uh, no, I think I'm fine.

GALBRAITH   *(considering)* Three, four years into your Ph.D. Middle of your thesis, three tutorials, this little office, working until all hours, you haven't been attending the conference, leaving me a series of phone and email messages about one undergraduate paper.

Beat.

JEFFREY   If you're suggesting / that—

GALBRAITH   Because it's inadvisable to throw around words like sexist, all right Jeffrey? Given the current climate in campus politics. And, once you've been in the department a little longer, then you'll start to—

JEFFREY   What? Then I'll what? I'll start referring to my female students as girls and allowing the attractive ones to write personal responses instead of essays. "How do you feel about Napoleon, Pixie?" "Oh, I really like him." B minus!

GALBRAITH   *(laughs)* No, but, over time, you will come to realize that students such as Pixie float through here every year on their way to the cultural studies department. Next year she'll switch to commerce, business admin. Why? Because she likes their building better. And then, when you've seen enough Pixies come and go, you'll realize it's best to just let them have their little say.

A momentary standoff between the men. PIXIE enters at the doorway.

PIXIE   Hi! Sorry to interrupt. *(to GALBRAITH)* Hi Professor. *(to JEFFREY)* I just wanted to let you know I'm here. If you're – uh – in the middle of something, I'll just wait in the hallway until you're—

GALBRAITH   No, Pixie, please, come in.

PIXIE   I can just wait in the hallway.

GALBRAITH   No, no, please, come in. Jeffrey and I were just discussing, but please.

JEFFREY   Uh, yes. Come in Pixie.

> *PIXIE enters.*

PIXIE   Am I in trouble… or…?

JEFFREY   Uh no, no Pixie, I'm sorry, please sit down—

PIXIE   Okay, just with the two of you standing there…

JEFFREY   Yes, I'm sorry, we were just finishing up. *(to PROFESSOR GALBRAITH)* Professor, I asked Pixie here to talk about her essay.

GALBRAITH   Right, right.

JEFFREY   And so I think I should, uh—

GALBRAITH   Right. Well, I'm off. I'll leave you to it.

> *Beat.*

Jeffrey, the conference resumes at ten tomorrow morning, should you choose to grace us. *(to PIXIE)* Pixie. Nice to see you again so soon.

PIXIE   Yeah.

GALBRAITH   And the assignment we discussed…? When was it, a week, a week and a half ago?

PIXIE   Yeah.

GALBRAITH   How did it go? Hm? Did you enjoy writing it?

PIXIE   *(with a quick glance at JEFFREY)* I, yes, I really enjoyed – I learned a lot.

GALBRAITH   That's good. That's good. That's very good.

> *GALBRAITH looks at JEFFREY. So does PIXIE, causing JEFFREY to turn away. Beat.*

There are sources, Pixie, that suggest Elizabeth Farnese may have led the Spanish Army against the French in 1717, not long after her accession.

PIXIE   Yeah, I came across that.

GALBRAITH   *(picturing it)* On horseback, at the head of the Spanish Army, as the formidable Louis XV crossed the Pyrenees.

PIXIE   Yes.

GALBRAITH   Quite the – quite the—

PIXIE   Yeah—

GALBRAITH   —feat! For a young…!

PIXIE   *(with a quick glance at JEFFREY)* Unhunh, yeah, I thought so too.

GALBRAITH   A very ambitious young person. Shared a number of qualities with Napoleon Bonaparte.

PIXIE   Uh, yeah! The comparison is kind of a stretch, of course. Napoleon conquered Europe, and Elizabeth got her sons thrones through her diplomacy, but, um, I think it holds.

GALBRAITH   *(considering her)* Elizabeth Farnese! It's a shame she wasn't allowed to cultivate her talents more fully. But, in the eighteenth century—

PIXIE   Yeah! I, uh—it's weird. There's not a lot of, um, women in this history we're covering—

GALBRAITH   No.

PIXIE   No, and the funny thing is, all term I've had this feeling of being left out. Like, it's all been very interesting, but it doesn't feel like it's about me, or for me, if that makes any sense?

> *GALBRAITH smiles at her.*

I thought it might just be because I'm in first year, and everything is a little…! But I think it's actually the content of the course. *(to JEFFREY)* And I was thinking about, uh, what you asked. Why – why I chose Elizabeth, why I wanted to write on her, and I think that probably, without realizing it, I chose her because – I don't know.

> *Beat.*

(to JEFFREY) Because I wanted to be in it, you know?

Beat.

GALBRAITH   Well, that's very nice, Pixie. That's a very nice sentiment.

PIXIE   Uh, yeah.

Beat.

JEFFREY   And Pixie, now that you've written on Elizabeth Farnese, do you feel there is a place for women in history? Or, are they just left out?

Beat.

PIXIE   Uh, um—

GALBRAITH   I'm sorry, Pixie. We're interrogating you. *(to JEFFREY)* Jeffrey, we're interrogating her, I think we should stop.

PIXIE   No, I just didn't, uh, come prepared to—

GALBRAITH   No, of course you didn't—

JEFFREY   I – I'm sorry Pixie, just the one last question, if you don't mind, and then we'll talk about your essay.

Beat.

PIXIE   What was the question?

GALBRAITH   Jeffrey, this is getting a little heavy-handed—

JEFFREY   The question was, is there a place for women in history?

Beat.

PIXIE   Well, from the lectures and the textbooks, I would say women don't have a place in history. But I don't know if I believe that.

JEFFREY   What do you believe?

Beat.

PIXIE   Is this about my essay?

GALBRAITH   All right, we've asked our questions. I think we should stop now before Pixie begins to feel put upon—

JEFFREY   *(a little too vehement)* She – no – she wants to answer!

> *Beat.*

> I – I'm sorry, is there some reason why Pixie shouldn't be allowed to offer a response?

> *Beat.*

GALBRAITH   Pixie, would you please wait in the hallway for a moment—

PIXIE   Uh, okay—

JEFFREY   *(motioning for PIXIE to wait)* Uh, no, Pixie. *(to GALBRAITH)* Professor, why? Is there some reason why Pixie can't answer?

GALBRAITH   She can answer, Jeffrey, it's not a question of whether or not she can answer—

JEFFREY   Then—

GALBRAITH   I have no objections to hearing Pixie's response—

JEFFREY   Then, good! Let's—

GALBRAITH   —but I'm afraid we're overburdening her—

JEFFREY   With one question?

> *Beat.*

GALBRAITH   *(to PIXIE)* Pixie, I'm sorry, if you could please wait in the hallway for one moment—

PIXIE   Uh, okay—

JEFFREY   I don't see why Pixie should wait in the hallway—

GALBRAITH   *(to PIXIE)* Jeffrey and I are… *(laughs)*—

JEFFREY   *(to GALBRAITH)* —while we—

GALBRAITH   *(to PIXIE)* —in the midst of a…. Your essay raised a number of questions—

JEFFREY   *(to PIXIE)* —about women and their under-representation in the historical record, and, Pixie, your essay interests us in that—

GALBRAITH   *(low, to JEFFREY)* Jeffrey—

JEFFREY   *(to PIXIE)* —in that it speaks to the deficit of female
      figures—

GALBRAITH   *(low, to JEFFREY)* I'd really prefer if you didn't—

JEFFREY   *(to PIXIE)* —as well as history departments' traditional
      unwillingness to—

GALBRAITH   *(to JEFFREY)* —extend our argument into
      student affairs!

JEFFREY   *(to GALBRAITH)* Extend it into…! It's about her. Her
      essay is the subject of the argument!

      Beat.

GALBRAITH   *(to PIXIE)* Thank you, Pixie, it will just be one
      minute.

PIXIE   Okay—

JEFFREY   *(to GALBRAITH)* Just now, Professor, Pixie very clear-
      ly expressed feelings of exclusion. She's been left out. The
      subject matter doesn't seem to be addressed to her—

GALBRAITH   Yes, I heard her—

JEFFREY   —the history excludes her.

GALBRAITH   I heard her.

JEFFREY   I'd like to – can we hear her out? Because I don't see
      how she can be included in the discourse if she's sitting in
      the hallway.

      Beat.

GALBRAITH   Fine, go ahead.

      JEFFREY stares at GALBRAITH.

Go ahead.

      GALBRAITH indicates that JEFFREY can ask his question.

JEFFREY   Pixie, I'm sorry, the question, should women have
      a place in history? I would very much like to hear your
      response.

Beat.

PIXIE Look, I – I don't know, okay? You're the experts. Why don't you tell me. I came here to learn, to be taught, so I really don't know.

Beat.

JEFFREY Yes—

PIXIE You're the experts.

JEFFREY Yes, we are, but, we're asking you because you wrote on Elizabeth Farnese, and, arguably, that makes you an expert. An Elizabeth Farnese expert.

PIXIE Okay, but that's a pretty limited, um, field, Elizabeth Farnese. And you asked me if women should be in history?

JEFFREY Yes.

PIXIE I think Elizabeth Farnese should be in history, is that what you're asking me?

Beat.

JEFFREY Well, Pixie, yes, okay, that's – yes, Elizabeth Farnese is part of this because you appealed your essay topic to Professor Galbraith, and that was a very strong gesture on your part, and it indicates to me that you are embracing feminist – but I'd like to broaden our discussion from – and talk about what you said a moment ago – that while taking this course history seemed closed to, or seemed to leave out, women.

Beat.

PIXIE Yeah?

JEFFREY And you said, I don't know if I believe that.

Beat.

PIXIE Yeah?

JEFFREY And you meant… what?

Beat. PIXIE shifts, thinks.

All right. Pixie, look, the essay topic, military leader, Elizabeth Farnese is not a military leader.

PIXIE   Well—

JEFFREY   Yes! Exactly! You questioned that! And I think this is important, because what you hit upon, Pixie, is that there's a certain amount of exclusivity, a certain sexism built into the terminology, into the wording of the essay questions, which are, of course, formulated by Professor Galbraith.

> *JEFFREY looks at PROFESSOR GALBRAITH, who looks away.*

And I think this relates to what you said a moment ago, about the textbooks, and the lectures—

PIXIE   —okay—

JEFFREY   —about your growing awareness of the emphasis on male figures—

PIXIE   —okay—

JEFFREY   *(half to GALBRAITH)* —and of the almost complete absence of female figures—

PIXIE   Yeah, okay—

JEFFREY   —and of the feelings of exclusion generated by what is a pronounced bias in the course material—

PIXIE   —unhunh—

JEFFREY   —as well as your skepticism. Your sense that women are a part of history—

PIXIE   *(soft)* —unhunh—

JEFFREY   —and that – that they would be a part of history if they weren't being under-represented in Professor Galbraith's lectures and on Professor Galbraith's course lists, and that, Pixie, that is what I'd like to hear about!

> *Beat.*

PIXIE   Why are you yelling at me?

JEFFREY   I'm not…! *(dropping the intensity level)* I'm not yelling, I'm trying to—

PIXIE   I, no, I don't want to answer this anymore.

>   *Beat.*

JEFFREY   No, Pixie, I'm sorry, let's – please, let's—

PIXIE   I feel uncomfortable answering this.

JEFFREY   But, but, Pixie—

GALBRAITH   Jeffrey—

JEFFREY   *(to GALBRAITH)* No. *(to PIXIE)* Pixie—

PIXIE   No. I don't want to—

JEFFREY   But…! Listen, let's just—

PIXIE   No.

GALBRAITH   Jeffrey—

JEFFREY   Look Pixie, let's just—

PIXIE   No.

JEFFREY   But, but Pixie!

PIXIE   You're yelling at me!

JEFFREY   I'm not – I'm not…! Pixie, just listen for one—

PIXIE   No.

JEFFREY   Just for one—

PIXIE   No.

JEFFREY   Please! Pixie! Just for one—

PIXIE   No, I – no. I don't care. I don't care about women in history, okay? This is my fucking elective. I have no idea!

>   *Beat.*

JEFFREY   You don't care.

>   *Beat.*

Doesn't it, for one second, occur to you that I am trying to defend you?

GALBRAITH   Jeffrey, I think we should stop now—

JEFFREY   That more is at stake than just your essay, and your grades—

GALBRAITH   Jeffrey, let's stop this right now.

JEFFREY   But, you know what, Pixie? Why don't you just glaze over—

GALBRAITH   —Jeffrey!—

JEFFREY   —while we determine that women and horses have equal historic significance! Or – or apply your fucking lip gloss one more time—

GALBRAITH   All right, Jeffrey!

JEFFREY   —while Professor Galbraith eliminates women from the historical record!

GALBRAITH   That's enough!

JEFFREY   You are being degraded and – and patronized—

GALBRAITH   That's enough, Jeffrey!

JEFFREY   —and you are sitting there like a lobotomized…! Like a lobotomy in a… skirt!

> *Long beat. Long enough for JEFFREY to contemplate the possible ramifications of his outburst. Very little motion occurs on stage. PIXIE begins to cry and covers her face.*

I – shit.

> *Beat.*

I – Pixie – I didn't – I didn't mean to – fuck.

> *Beat.*

I – I – fuck.

GALBRAITH   Hm, yes. Jeffrey? Would you please wait in the hallway for a moment?

JEFFREY *(half to GALBRAITH, half to PIXIE)* I – no, look, I – I'm sorry—

GALBRAITH Yes, I know you are—

JEFFREY I just got – I got—

GALBRAITH Yes, I know. But now I would prefer if you went out into the hallway.

JEFFREY But – I – Professor, I—

GALBRAITH Because, as you can see, Pixie is crying, and I think it would be best to give her a chance to collect herself.

> *JEFFREY doesn't go.*

Jeffrey?

JEFFREY I – yes, I just – I don't feel all that comfortable leaving her... with...

GALBRAITH The head of the department?

> *A standoff between the two men. Beat. PIXIE's crying is audible.*

All right, Jeffrey. Can we please offer Pixie some Kleenex?

> *JEFFREY gets a box of tissues off the bookshelf. GAL-BRAITH takes the box of tissues from JEFFREY, and goes over to PIXIE. She takes a couple of tissues without looking up. Long beat of crying.*

PIXIE I'm just trying to... *(gestures)...*

GALBRAITH Please. I think it would be very strange if you weren't crying. I would cry if the dean yelled at me.

> *GALBRAITH smiles at PIXIE. PIXIE tries to pull it together again. Another beat of crying.*

(with sympathy) You're upset.

> *PIXIE nods.*

PIXIE *(quiet)* Yeah.

GALBRAITH *(with sympathy)* Hm.

Beat.

I'm very sorry about this, Pixie. I shouldn't have let Jeffrey yell at you, I should have… stepped in. *(for JEFFREY's benefit)* This is not how we encourage our TA's to behave.

Beat.

Jeffrey hasn't been raising his voice in tutorial, has he?

PIXIE shakes her head no.

PIXIE   No.

GALBRAITH   No. Hm.

Beat.

You should know that we do have a formal complaints procedure at the university, Pixie. There is a women's coordinator. Or, rather, what is the current…?

Beat.

Jeffrey?

JEFFREY   Yes?

GALBRAITH   What's the new title for the women's coordinator?

JEFFREY   The equity officer?

GALBRAITH   The equity officer. *(to PIXIE)* She's in the Office of the Dean of Students. She's a very approachable person, and I'm sure she would help you make your case.

Beat.

One of the avenues of appeal, when incidents of this type occur, is to come and talk with me. We've bypassed that step, as I witnessed the incident. And, in my experience, handling these types of incidents in the department, I've found that it's important for the student to hear from the professor, or, in this case, TA, themselves. What's important for the student is to hear the faculty member acknowledge that their behaviour was not… appropriate. Then, hopefully, a teaching relationship can be re-established.

Beat.

I know Jeffrey would like to apologize to you. And I will be here supervising, so if anything makes you feel uncomfortable, then we'll stop, and I'll ask Jeffrey to leave.

Beat.

Hm? Pixie? Is that…?

PIXIE shrugs – sure. GALBRAITH smiles at her.

Jeffrey.

GALBRAITH indicates to JEFFREY that he should speak to PIXIE.

JEFFREY   *(half to GALBRAITH)* I – I – yes. I'm very sorry. I lost my – I uh – I shouldn't have used that language to—

GALBRAITH   *(sharp)* Are you apologizing to Pixie, Jeffrey?

JEFFREY   *(confused)* Yes?

GALBRAITH indicates that PIXIE is over there.

(to PIXIE) Pixie, I shouldn't have used—I was frustrated, and I chose the wrong words to express that—

PIXIE   You yelled at me!

JEFFREY   Yes. I – yes. I'm sorry.

PIXIE   I came here to get my essay. I came here to pick up my essay, so can I have it please, or are you on all crack?

JEFFREY   Yes, I – I know that this must seem—

PIXIE   You wanted to talk to me about my essay, that's what you said, that's why I came here, to talk about my essay! And then—

JEFFREY   Yes, I know, I see that—

PIXIE   —and then you YELL AT ME!!!

JEFFREY   I – yes, I appreciate that this isn't what you were expecting. You were expecting a formal discussion of your essay and your grade, but Pixie, we were, in fact, talking about your essay—

PIXIE   No we weren't. You were arguing with Professor Galbraith.

> *Beat.*

JEFFREY   *(quiet)* But… *(laughs)* …Pixie, yes, but—

PIXIE   You were arguing.

JEFFREY   Yes, but, what you don't understand is, I was trying to – I was advocating for you, because, you see—

PIXIE   You were in the middle of an argument! You and the Professor were arguing!

JEFFREY   But – yes – I – yes, but you see, the argument was..∴ about you.

PIXIE   No it wasn't!

JEFFREY   But you don't…! *(laughs)* It – it – yes, it was about… you—

PIXIE   No.

> *Beat.*

JEFFREY   But it – yes—

PIXIE   It wasn't about me!

> *Beat.*

JEFFREY   But – but, okay, Pixie—

PIXIE   This wasn't about me.

JEFFREY   But I was – I was advocating for you. I was trying to advocate for you. You – what do you want? I was trying to – what do you women fucking want!

GALBRAITH   Jeffrey!

JEFFREY   I was putting my – I was – fuck – I was advocating for women!

PIXIE   You were arguing with Professor Galbraith! You were arguing with him about women in history. I was just… in the room!

> *Beat.*

Which is so funny, because in the textbook – the reason – the reason why I wrote the essay is because in the textbook, at the bottom of one of the pages, there's a footnote. Elizabeth Farnese, second wife of Philip the Fifth of Spain, secured her sons the thrones of Parma and Tuscany. She got her sons thrones. How? It doesn't say. There's just the footnote. So I wrote the essay. And I was sitting here, looking at you, and I could tell you wanted me to say certain things for the sake of your argument, and I was thinking, my history TA is yelling at me for no reason and I am pissed off because I am kind of like a footnote here!

> *Beat.*

"Professor Galbraith and Jeffrey had an argument about whether or not women should be included in history. And by the way, they were arguing because of Pixie Findley." "Pixie Findley? Who's she?" "Let's check the footnote." And somehow, even though you think it's about me, it's not. It's about you. And your argument. I'm just the excuse for you to argue with each other. So I don't care which one of you wins because it's not about me.

> *Beat.*

So… yeah.

> *Long beat.*

JEFFREY   I see what you're… saying, but, Pixie, I didn't mean to…. It's – yes – you're talking about – yes, I see what you're pointing out, and I didn't mean to – to – I – you're right. I shouldn't have – I didn't, uh – I never, uh, asked you if you wanted me to – but my intention – my intention wasn't to appropriate, to – uh… yeah.

> *Beat.*

I'm – Pixie, I'm sorry.

Beat.

I'm… sorry.

PIXIE   That's okay.

JEFFREY   I'm sorry. You're right, I – yes. I was – yes.

PIXIE   That's okay.

GALBRAITH   Have we, perhaps, resolved this? Pixie?

PIXIE shrugs, nods.

PIXIE   Yeah.

GALBRAITH   Good, good. Good. Then perhaps we can leave this for now?

PIXIE   Yeah.

PIXIE picks up her bag and PROFESSOR GALBRAITH ushers her to the doorway over the course of his speech.

GALBRAITH   We have a lot to offer here in the history department, Pixie. Perhaps not as much as the business school – that's the large architectural tribute to Fort Knox and the Playboy Mansion up that way – but we have a lot to offer. And Pixie? Please come to me if you feel uncomfortable, or if you would like to discuss this further.

PIXIE   Okay. Thanks.

PIXIE exits. The men look after her for a moment. Beat.

GALBRAITH   Off she goes.

Long beat.

If you were tenured, Jeffrey, I would say, by all means, go ahead and yell gendered slurs at the female undergraduates. But, at this juncture in your career… *(laughs).*

Beat.

I appreciate that you wanted to argue your point to me. But we're the – you're a Ph.D. candidate, I'm a professor; distinguished, books published, summa cum laude, et cetera, et cetera. What could Pixie Findley possibly have contributed to our discussion? Hm?

Beat.

Connect up the dots for me.

JEFFREY   It started off with me trying to defend her—

GALBRAITH   *(sharp)* From?

JEFFREY   Yes, I – I – yes, I'm the one who insulted her, who verbally… insulted her, in a gendered – in a language that was – I don't know where I – how I – what made me—

GALBRAITH   Oh, for Christ's sake, the girl's name is Pixie! Her name is Pixie! She's asking to be patronized.

> *Beat.*

If you were to crack her skull open, butterflies would flutter out. Or, what did you say? Lobotomy in a skirt?

> *GALBRAITH laughs, regards JEFFREY, laughs again. JEFFREY stares at GALBRAITH.*

Lucky for you. Let's just pray she doesn't pick up Simone de Beauvoir over the weekend, hm?

> *Beat.*

Let's just pray she sticks to *Cosmopolitan*, or what is it my wife reads? *Vanity Fair.*

> *Beat.*

And Jeffrey? Give her a B minus.

> *GALBRAITH hands JEFFREY the essay and exits. JEFFREY holds it for a moment, then he opens it and begins to read. Lights out.*

USSR

USSR was first produced as part of a double bill with *The Russian Play* at Harbourfront Centre in January of 2007, with the following company:

ELENA   Maev Beaty

Director: Natasha Mytnowych
Set & Costume Design: Natasha Mytnowych with Camellia Koo
Lighting Design: Kimberly Purtell
Music Composition and Performance: Tom Howell
Assistant Director: Julia Lederer
Stage Manager: Joanna Barrotta

CHARACTERS

ELENA: twenty-five

ELENA speaks with a Russian accent.

USSR

ELENA, holding a cigarette, stands under a light bulb that hangs too low from its plastic fixture. She smokes, regarding the audience. She ashes her cigarette onto the linoleum floor. The background is indiscernible, dark.

ELENA   I haven't had a cigarette since I was pregnant with Mikhail. (*She looks at the cigarette.*) Well, that's not true, because I have this package in the freezer, so I am sometimes smoking, but only for special occasion.

>   *Beat.*

My mother, funny thing that my mother say when I was a little girl. She say to me, "Elena, there is only two types of wives. There is the type of wife who will cut up the children and feed them to her husband, and there is the type of wife who will cut up her husband and feed him to the children." So maybe this is not such a load of shit, after all, what my mother say.

>   *Beat.*

When I met Lee, my husband, Lee, I was twenty-one years old. I was medical student, living with my mother and father in old KGB housing not far from Kremlin. This KGB apartment building, I remember it because there was an elevator that was made of wood. Lee was very fascinated by the elevator. He would tell me I was a crazy person to smoke cigarettes in an elevator made of wood and wire, with sparks flying off it in all direction. Lee was wanting to know why it was not catching on fire, and I would say, "I don't know, luck?" Like everything in Moscow, held together by luck. Lee was always wanting to look at this elevator, but he couldn't because there was no light in the hallway, because other people living in this building would take the light bulbs. For ten light bulbs you could get bottle of vodka, so people took them.

>   *Beat.*

We would rather have vodka than light in Moscow.

Beat.

I met Lee because – it was because of a friend, Irina. She
lived with her grandfather over McDonald's, trying to
run small internet business with smell of hamburgers
always in the hallway. Irina was meeting with American
men. She was always saying to me, she was going to
dance club for Western men, and she would say, "Come
and meet the Americans, you won't believe how they will
spend so much money!" That made me have curiosity for
what it would be like in the Western club.

Beat.

Club had little bit of sex atmosphere, I have to admit this
to you. But, Lee was not – he was in Moscow for business
reasons. He was investor for company, looking to buy oil
industry in Russia. He told me he liked Russia because
he liked watching switch to free market economy, is interesting economic experiment taking place on Russian
people, he said. I told Lee we had word for this, for to
explain what was happening in politics, word for privati-
zation and for grabbing put together, in Russian something
like grabicization. This made Lee laugh. So right from
the beginning Lee was talking about business with me.
Lee was not thinking I was stupid about these things,
economics, politics so you see I was not just stuffed doll
asking Lee what is my opinion? I was not just stupid
Russian girl with no hope of prospect, saying only yes
please to Western man.

Beat.

My English was not so hot at this time, not so basic as
Irina, who is only saying things like apple juice and have
a good night, but still basic, and Lee's Russian is total
shit. So sometime we were just saying each other's name,
just saying Lee Lee Lee, Elena Elena Elena, to each other,
like a love poem with only two words in it.

Beat. ELENA puts out the cigarette, thinks.

I don't know! When I think about it, it's hard for me
to tell you what was love for Lee, and what was desire to

leave Russia, hard to tell the difference in my emotions.
I know it was nice quality that he was Canadian. Very
nice quality of Lee, Canadian passport. Because look at
this example of Russia! Doctors were not making enough
for soap, television, but in Moscow, prostitute are some of
the richest persons because they are paid in American
dollars. I should have been training to be prostitute, not
doctor, if I was having financial consideration. And old
people were selling their drug in the streets, this was
typical problem, and the fighting in Chechnya, and the
grabicization that was happening in all possible direction.

   Beat.

And my – my uh – my – I was in love—stupid—I was
young woman, and I was in love with this person who
died, fighting in Chechnya. Well, not fighting, was just
killed by Chechen who paid off to Russian army, but
anyway, that is not official story.

   Beat.

So Canada! Canada was like place of…! When I first come
here, I would sit and watch the television and there
would be report on dog who fell into frozen river, and the
police were not able to get the dog out. This was big
emergency on the news here in Toronto.

   Beat.

I have, to my mind, all normal feeling of love toward Lee.
But for Toronto persons, it was not…. I would tell to
Toronto persons, "I am Russian woman with Canadian
husband." And in their look, I would see them thinking,
"Ah! This is the Russian brides that come off the internet!"
This not very welcoming reaction is typical of Toronto
persons, and so it was difficult to—I—my friends in
Toronto were not, uh – there was a person named Sergei
from Russia, from – not Moscow, but outside of Moscow,
taxi driver who I met with in Toronto.

   Beat.

In Russia, my English seem okay because is better than
most people! But in Toronto, I was just another ESL person
slowing things down, asking stupid questions. So it was
hard to make friendships with Toronto persons for this
reason also, but anyway, I don't like to think about this
stupid – stupid friendship I had with Sergei, because it
was actually part of moving to Toronto, not a good reflection
of myself, but worst part of person making decision from
homesick feeling, so I haven't like to think about it
because of – because of my son, Mikhail. (*She says the
name with a Canadian accent.*) Michael. Speaking perfect
English, my son. Michael. He is the most beautiful, special
person I have ever met, and not even two years old, can
you believe?

    Beat.

When I see Mikhail for the first time in the hospital, I am
thinking, thank God for my Canadian husband, and
I am feeling such a love for Lee, and also for this big cold
country that is not Russia, because of Mikhail. Little person
who is mine and not mine, belonging to Canada also,
with big, beautiful blue eyes looking at me over the top of
the blanket, that are then later slowly turning brown.

    Beat.

Lee was so happy, so…! Russian men are not happy like
this about babies, let me tell you.

    Beat.

I did know something was not—that there was a possibility
of—because of course, I study genetic, so this is a question
in my mind. But just a little question, because I don't like
to think that this friendship with Sergei that was sometime taking place in the back of the taxi was – that this
friendship was…. And I am not seeing Sergei after
Mikhail is born, plus also, this was almost three years
ago, so I don't like to think about it very much.

    Beat.

This was time of happiness, so I didn't…

ELENA lights another cigarette and continues to ash onto the floor. She regards the audience. Beat.

I have my class for entrance at University of Toronto. This is why I don't go with Lee to the business dinner.

I forget what exactly it was for, but I know at the party, a friend of Lee who is a doctor, he say to Lee something about Mikhail's eyes. Lee and him are just joking together and then he say something that is half joke but also have a question in it, something like it is not usual for brown-eyed son with blue-eyed father and mother. Possible on outside chance of genetic, but not typical. I'm not at this party so I don't find this out at the time. So, this is why Lee is on his knees beside Mikhail and looking at him so closely when I come home tonight.

    Beat.

I know what I should have said, now I can think. I should have said something like, "Please, Lee, you are crazy to say this thing," with such a confidence to him. But I don't say this, I just stand there with no answer. This is my brain that is slow in English language for you. So then Lee is yelling and yelling, yelling things at me like fuck you, and I am also yelling things that are a little bit crazy. I am saying to him, "Why didn't you ever learn Russian, you can't even know my real self, because my real self is Russian, and you need Russian language for that." And I am yelling at him about this elevator in Moscow, made of wood, and Lee couldn't understand it because it is a Russian elevator. How can he understand me when he can't even understand an elevator and I am a person? And I am yelling in Russian some of this and he is yelling, "Speak English, you cunt," at me, and also he is crying.

    Beat.

Lee is yelling in my face, and I am thinking I am sorry for this. I am sorry, and I love you, and Sergei was just home-sick feeling I was having for Russia, but Lee is so angry and yelling, so I don't say this, I just wait there with my hand over my face, waiting. Then Lee pick up Mikhail, but not uh—he pick him up by his clothing, and

Mikhail's head fall back on his neck, and I am screaming at Lee to put Mikhail down, and he is screaming, "Who was it, who was it, some Russian asshole."

Beat.

Lee is not looking at Mikhail, and Mikhail is choking because of the way Lee is holding him, so I am trying to get Mikhail from Lee. Lee has him away from my hand, saying again, "Who was it who was it who was it who was it," so I pick up a ashtray from off the table and I...

Beat.

I don't know why I...

Beat.

I just hit him like that with the ashtray from the table, on the back of his neck—by then he is on the ground.

Beat.

I carry Mikhail away into the other room, away from this fighting. Mikhail is not even crying, just with big eyes looking at me. I put him down and I come back, and Lee is...

Beat.

And I am saying, "Lee, please, don't lie there, don't be stupid, is dirty and cold on the floor, so please get up."

Beat.

But he don't, he—stupid—he don't – he just, uh...

The pool of light broadens, has been broadening, so we see LEE, lying very still and face down, on the periphery of the light. A heavy glass ashtray lies near him. ELENA turns for the first time and looks behind her. She turns back.

So this is not great advertising for Russian wife.

Beat.

This is not going to make you believe me when I say to you that I did love Lee, and that I was a happy person with my Canadian husband.

Lights out.

MEXICO CITY

Mexico City was first presented as part of the inaugural Lab Cab Festival in Toronto, in September of 2006, with the following company:

HENRY   Brendan Gall
ALICE   Maev Beaty

Director: Alan Dilworth

Mexico City premiered at the SummerWorks Theatre Festival in Toronto on August 3rd, 2007, with the following company:

HENRY   Brendan Gall
ALICE   Molly Atkinson

Director: Alan Dilworth
Set & Costume Design: Camellia Koo & Anna Treusch
Lighting Design: Kimberly Purtell
Sound Design: Thomas Ryder Payne
Stage Manager: Liz Air

CHARACTERS

HENRY: late twenties, tall and lanky, a little sullen
ALICE: mid twenties, full-figured and beautiful, a little high-
    pitched

MEXICO CITY

*Lights up on HENRY and ALICE. They are holding
a fixed pose as though a photograph is being taken of
them. Mariachi music plays as they address the audience.*

HENRY   It was his idea to vacation in Mexico—

ALICE   —but she liked the idea very much. After all, they hadn't
taken a holiday together since their honeymoon, and that
was 1957, going on three years past, would you believe?

HENRY   Oh, he believed it!

ALICE looks at HENRY.

He thought a holiday would be nice. It would shake them
up, shake them out of their routines.

Beat.

Liven things up a little.

Beat.

He booked off a weeks' vacation from the small architecture
firm where he worked.

ALICE   She purchased a copy of a tour book, and an account of
Mexican travels titled, somewhat ironically, *Poor Mexico,
so far from God and so close to the United States!*

HENRY   He found an old Spanish phrase book and set to
memory a few essential lines.

ALICE   *Buenos tardes.* Good afternoon.

HENRY   *Quanto?* How much?

ALICE   *Cuarto de baño.* Restroom.

HENRY   He felt they ought to have found a kennel for the dog.

ALICE   But her sister had offered to look after him.

HENRY   Of course, his wife's sister wasn't the most reliable of
girls—

ALICE   —which is why she should be allowed to walk the dog.
How else was she supposed to learn responsibility?

Beat.

HENRY   Because his wife could be such a determined woman—

ALICE   —and he himself, it must be conceded, could also be very difficult at times—

HENRY   —the planning of the vacation led to several disagreements.

ALICE   She wanted to visit some of Mexico City's world-class art galleries—

HENRY   —but he objected. He would like to go up north to the desert region, on a sort of expedition into the wild.

ALICE   She felt that the artistic works of the likes of Frida Kahlo and Diego Rivera should not be brushed aside so unfeelingly.

HENRY   But he was sick of being dragged around galleries. That's all they ever did on their honeymoon, drag around galleries. Three days at the Louvre, a day and a half at the Musée d'Art Moderne—

ALICE   How could he say that? He had loved the Louvre. He had loved the Louvre just as much as she had.

HENRY   He had been pretending. To please her.

ALICE   What kind of a boor couldn't appreciate art?

Beat.

But, there was one point about which they were both in complete agreement. They would not join a package tour—

HENRY   —but would rough it by themselves.

ALICE   After all, they were in pursuit of the authentic Mexico—

HENRY   —the undiluted Mexico—

ALICE   —the real Mexico.

Beat.

HENRY   The plane ride was uneventful.

ALICE   She tried to read her tour book on the plane, but she just couldn't keep her eyes open.

HENRY   He spent his time ordering gin and tonics and trying out his Spanish on one of the air flight stewardesses.

ALICE   Of course, the air flight stewardess couldn't understand him.

HENRY   How would she know, she had been sleeping.

ALICE   She kept waking up. Every time the poor girl misunderstood him.

HENRY   If she hadn't been sleeping, then why had her mouth been gaping open, and spit dripping out of it?

ALICE   What a despicable thing to say to someone.

HENRY   She had provoked him. Anyone who was listening would agree she had provoked him.

ALICE   Henry, you are such a—

HENRY   What? What Alice? What am I? Please, I'd really love to know.

> HENRY and ALICE turn back to the audience, embarrassed. Beat.

ALICE   The hotel where they were staying was charming.

HENRY   It was very grand.

ALICE   She told her husband that the decor was signature Mexican, and these were very Mexican colours.

HENRY   At which point, he reminded her that they were in Mexico, and while the hotel room was very Mexican, so was Mexico, and he'd like to see some of it.

ALICE   They set out in the direction of the town square.

HENRY   The *zócalo*.

ALICE   It was nearing noon, the hottest part of the day. The dogs on the sidewalk were sleeping so soundly it seemed as though they were dead. Perhaps they were dead. She would just run over and check.

HENRY   The dogs were not dead. They were perfectly fine, now could they get a move on?

> *Beat.*

ALICE   On the way to the town square, they passed by several taco stands. Girls in wide straw hats and soiled skirts were frying bread and meat on an open grill.

HENRY   There were bowls of onions and green chili sauces—

ALICE   —that smelled not quite fresh—

HENRY   —but he was hungry, so he stopped in front of a stand and reached into his money belt for a few pesos.

ALICE   While they were standing there, a piece of meat fell away from the bone, and she realized that it was a pig's head being blackened on the grill. She could see the animal's teeth, and the bristles on its head were smouldering. Its eyeballs had fallen loose in their sockets and were dangling down its snout.

HENRY   He wasn't so much put off by the pig's head as by the dark passage behind the taco stand. There was a pile of meat lying in the back of a truck, baking in the sun, and the dog below it was jumping up and chewing on whatever it could reach.

ALICE   She reminded her husband that the tour book said not to eat street food, and in big block letters it warned—

HENRY   —don't drink the water. But he was hungry, and the meat was cooked, and in any case, he had a strong stomach. He bought a taco and wolfed it down while the dogs nearby shook themselves awake and began circling around him and whining.

ALICE   She bought a soda and some crackers from a corner store. She thought that perhaps they ought to find a pharmacy and purchase some antacid, just in case he—

HENRY   He would be fine! The meat had been cooked! Nothing was going to happen to him!

ALICE   Well, she hoped he was right.

HENRY   He was right!

ALICE   Well, she certainly hoped so!

> *Beat.*

It was just then that they happened into the market.

HENRY   It was off the town square, down the narrow colonial streets, unchanged since the Spanish had conquered the Aztecs some four hundred years previous.

ALICE   The market was packed with people, and as they pushed their way in—

HENRY   —they held onto their cameras and purses.

ALICE   They were shoulder to shoulder with Mexicans!

HENRY   Well, he wasn't, he was taller than them, by a foot in most cases.

ALICE   She was surrounded by dark hair and dark eyes, men in shabby suits and women carrying babies with blankets thrown over them.

HENRY   He raised his camera several times but the picture was moving too fast.

ALICE   She was so close she could smell the people as they passed her.

HENRY   The smell of beer and corn—

ALICE   —and the raw, sweet scent of densely packed bodies sweating in the sun.

> *Beat.*

HENRY   He noticed his wife's presence was attracting a lot of attention. The men, most of them standing around waiting for sales—

ALICE   —were pointing her out to each other—

HENRY   —and making certain hand gestures that were impossible to misunderstand. He felt a sort of uneasiness rise in him. He was right there, after all, and it was clear this was his wife.

ALICE   Although she couldn't understand all of what was
being said about her, she distinguished the word for
foreigner. *Gringa.*

HENRY   And the word for skirt. And wasn't that the word
for…?

    HENRY is horrified.

He pulled his wife out of the market—

ALICE   —Henry!—

HENRY   —down a dark alley—

ALICE   —Henry, where are you taking us?—

HENRY   —and into a church.

    Beat.

ALICE   Was the market too authentic for you, darling?

    ALICE smiles. HENRY looks away.

HENRY   The church was filled with candles and old women
praying aloud in Spanish, and there was a gold-toothed
gypsy washing her baby in the baptismal font—

ALICE   —and a little girl sitting in the doorway selling
Madonna figurines and shelling peas into a basket.

HENRY   (*reading from the tour book*) The Church of the Blood of
our Christ, built by Spanish conquistadors in 1682—

ALICE   —was a mass of grimy black stones, permeated with
the smell of incense and engraved with Latin epitaphs
commemorating the Catholic dead.

HENRY   They sat in one of the pews together and looked up at
the altarpiece.

ALICE   It was Jesus on the cross, his hand and foot wounds
bleeding heavily. The blood from his crown of thorns was
dripping down onto his face and shoulders. She whis-
pered to her husband that this was similar to late-
medieval crucifixion tableaux.

HENRY   Well, whatever it was, it was very bloody-minded.

ALICE   She told her husband not to be ridiculous, it wasn't
         bloody-minded, it was art.

HENRY   Bloody-minded art.

ALICE   And just then, when she was about to remind him that
         art could only be appreciated when it was properly
         understood—

HENRY   —and just when he was about to remind her not to
         lecture him—

ALICE   —a priest emerged from the shadowy recesses of the
         church. He looked at them disapprovingly. He started
         gesturing, and speaking to them in Spanish.

HENRY   What the hell was he saying, something about a shirt?

ALICE   Or her arms? Was it her arms?

HENRY   *Corto...? Corto...?*

ALICE   *Menja...?* Is he saying *menja*? Or *manga*?

HENRY   Oh Christ, he's saying short sleeves, they're not
         allowed in the church.

ALICE   The priest ushered them to the entrance, pointed to
         a very dirty sign, in Spanish, which was nailed to the
         door—

HENRY   —"No bare feet. No uncovered arms"—

ALICE   —and then waved them away.

         Beat.

         Well. That wasn't very Christian of him.

HENRY   "So far from God!"

         Beat.

ALICE   The best thing to do would be to take a look in the tour
         book and see what else was in the vicinity. She was sure
         there was an Aztec temple off the main square.

HENRY   Yes, yes, the... what-d'you-call-it?

ALICE   The Temple.

HENRY   No, in Mexican!

ALICE   How on earth was she supposed to know? She wasn't Mexican! Why didn't he ask one of the Mexicans!

HENRY   Why was she was getting all het up?

ALICE   She wasn't getting all het up! She was hot and dusty, and her shoes were beginning to cramp, and she didn't have the slightest idea where they were!

HENRY   He knew where they were!

ALICE   Well then, where were they, exactly?

HENRY   He knew where they were, now would she calm down already!

ALICE   She was perfectly calm!

HENRY   She was making a scene!

ALICE   I am not making a scene. How dare you, Henry!

HENRY   You're always making a scene, Alice! You're never happy unless you're making a scene!

> *HENRY gestures towards the audience. HENRY and ALICE stop fighting and turn back to the audience, but this time, as well as being embarrassed, they both resent the audience's presence. HENRY taps his foot and looks away. ALICE fixes her hair.*

May I have the guidebook, please?

> *Beat. ALICE hands it to him reluctantly.*

He took the guidebook out of his wife's hands. He led her back through the market, through the town square, and all the way to the Aztec Temple.

ALICE   It was a labyrinth of yellow stone walls.

HENRY   He bought tickets from a heavy-lidded Mexican with a waxed moustache, and they wandered in, past the massive cracked columns—

ALICE   —and the collapsed vaults—

HENRY   —in the direction of the famed altarpiece.

ALICE   As they walked along the narrow stone passageways, she noticed the walls had skulls engraved into them—

HENRY   —and ancient hieroglyphs.

ALICE   She wondered what they meant.

HENRY   Beware, probably.

    Beat.

ALICE   At the centre of the long, winding corridors, a set of well-worn stone steps led to the altar.

HENRY   The steps were bordered on all sides by a deep groove, a little like a gutter, cut into the rock. He read to his wife from the tour book that, once the hearts were cut out, the bodies of the sacrificial victims were thrown down the stairs. That's what the gutters were for. For the blood! What a marvel of architecture! Gutters for the blood!

ALICE   How did they cut the hearts out?

HENRY   Oh, a sharpened stone, most likely.

ALICE   A sharpened stone?

HENRY   Most likely.

ALICE   She felt a faint cold chill run down her back. She pulled on her husband's shirt and suggested they find their way out to the gift shop.

HENRY   But he was reluctant to leave. Didn't she want to see the rack of skulls, the chamber where the hearts, still pulsing with blood, were displayed?

ALICE   No, she certainly did not! She thought it was beastly!

HENRY   It's not beastly, it's architecture.

ALICE   It's…! Henry, they ripped one another's hearts out. It's beastly!

HENRY   What? Is it too authentic for you, darling?

ALICE   Yes! Yes Henry, it's too authentic for me! Mexico is too authentic for me, now can we please…!

    ALICE stops. She holds her hand out.

Oh no, it's raining. Oh, Henry, it's raining!

> *HENRY pulls up his collar and ALICE holds her purse over her head.*

Oh no, oh my skirt, my hair, my—

HENRY At first, it seemed it would only last a minute, so he pulled his wife under a ledge of stone to wait it out. But the rain kept pouring down on them.

ALICE A warm deluge of rain that turned the parched stone corridor into a canal—

HENRY —cascaded down the yellow walls—

ALICE —and trickled over the ledge under which they were standing, dripping onto their necks and the backs of their legs.

> *Beat.*

She told her husband she was getting very wet.

HENRY He gritted his teeth, and told her he was getting very wet too.

ALICE Well, then why didn't they turn back?

HENRY Because they didn't know it was going to rain!

ALICE She was turning back right now!

HENRY No she wasn't!

ALICE Yes she was, and he couldn't stop her!

HENRY Could she please try to stop being such a snit!

ALICE A snit!? A snit!?

HENRY Oh, for crying out loud! They were in Mexico City, goddamn it. They had come all this way. They were, at this moment, standing at the very centre of the ancient Aztec empire. Now, could she at least please pretend to enjoy herself!

ALICE She hated Mexico!!! She hated it! It was a horrible country! Why would anyone want to come here! It was like one of those short stories on the radio, where the locals turn out to be savages with big pots to boil you in or sacrifice you to the Sun God when you just wanted to have a nice trip! A nice trip, Henry! And it's been terrible, all we've done is argue, and you know I hate to argue with you—

HENRY   You hate to argue with me!?

ALICE   Yes, of course I do!

HENRY   You love to argue with me! It's your favourite thing. You're always arguing with me, day in and day out. Crab, crab, crab!

ALICE   Henry!

HENRY   Crab, crab, crab! As though it's my fault it's raining!

ALICE   If you don't shut up, I'm going to lose my wits, Henry!

HENRY   If you don't shut up, I'm going to cut your heart out and throw you down those stairs!

> *Beat.*

ALICE   And just then, when the whole trip seemed as though it was ruined, when she wished Mexico City and her husband were at the bottom of the ocean—

HENRY   —when he wished he could trade his wife for a shot of tequila and a plane ride home—

ALICE   —they heard a sound.

> *Beat.*

HENRY   What the hell is that?

ALICE   The sound of... was it... crying?

HENRY   They stood together and listened.

> *Beat.*

ALICE   A... is it a... child? Moaning? Or singing?

HENRY   Or a dog?

ALICE   What if someone's in danger, Henry!

HENRY   He took hold of his wife's hand and led her out into the rain.

ALICE   Oh no, my skirt.

HENRY   They waded along the narrow passageways in the direction of the sounds—

ALICE   —Oh, be careful, Henry! —

HENRY   —turned a corner, and through a veil of rain, they saw…

> *HENRY and ALICE try to see through the rain. Beat.*

It was the Mexican with the waxed moustache who had sold them the entrance tickets—

ALICE   —and a very pretty Mexican girl with long black hair and dark eyes.

HENRY   They were clutching each other and leaning up against a wall.

ALICE   Her head was thrown back and her mouth was open.

HENRY   His eyes were closed.

ALICE   And, oh my God, her skirt was pulled up to her—

HENRY   His trousers were down around his—

ALICE   And she was—

HENRY   He was—

ALICE   They were…! Were they even married?

HENRY   I don't think so, darling. They don't look as though they're married at all!

> *HENRY and ALICE watch the couple.*

ALICE   We shouldn't be watching, Henry.

HENRY   At least not both at once.

ALICE   Henry!

HENRY   Sh! They'll hear!

> *HENRY and ALICE watch the couple.*

(*soft*) Well, my dear.

ALICE   (*soft*) What, Henry?

HENRY   (*soft*) I think we've found the real Mexico.

> *Beat.*

> There it is.

> *Beat.*

ALICE   Sometimes, Henry, you say the most beautiful things.

HENRY   Do I?

ALICE   Yes.

HENRY   Alice, do you know what the most beautiful thing I've seen in Mexico City is?

ALICE   No?

HENRY   You. You, just as you are, standing in the rain.

ALICE   Really.

HENRY   Oh yes.

> *HENRY and ALICE kiss. They pause for a moment and look out at the audience. They hesitate. Should they ignore us? They turn back and kiss each other more passionately. Slow lights down with a reprise of the mariachi music.*

photo by Ian Brown

HANNAH MOSCOVITCH is a Toronto-based writer. Her first full-length play, *East of Berlin*, recently premiered at Tarragon Theatre and will be remounted at Tarragon as part of the 2008-2009 season. Hannah is a graduate of the National Theatre School of Canada.